CAMPING WITH KIDS IN CALIFORNIA

The Complete Guide

Where to Go and What to Do
for a Fun-Filled, Stress-Free
Camping Vacation

Bill McMillon

PRIMA PUBLISHING

To Mom, who made camping a part of our family life.

© 1996 by Bill McMillon

PRIMA PUBLISHING and colophon are trademarks of Prima Communications, Inc.

Library of Congress Cataloging-in-Publication Data

McMillon, Bill, 1942-
  Camping with kids in California: the complete guide—where to go and what to do for a fun-filled, stress-free camping vacation / Bill McMillon.

        p.   cm.
    Includes index.
    ISBN 0-7615-0003-0
    1. Camping—California. 2. Family recreation—California. 3. Campsites, facilities. etc—California—Directories. I. Title.
GV191.42.C2M35 1995
796.54—dc20   95-2141
                                                        CIP

96 97 98 99 00 AA 10 9 8 7 6 5 4 3 2 1
Printed in the United States of America

How to Order:
Single copies may be ordered from Prima Publishing, P.O. Box 1260BK, Rocklin, CA 95677; telephone (916) 632-4400. Quantity discounts are also available. On your letterhead, include information concerning the intended use of the books and the number of books you wish to purchase.

CONTENTS

Acknowledgments   v

Introduction   vii

Tips for Camping with Kids   1

How to Use This Guide   15

SECTION 1: OUTSTANDING CAMPGROUNDS FOR KIDS

1. North Coast Camping   19
2. North Inland Camping   71
3. Central Coast Camping   123
4. Central Inland Camping   143
5. South Coast Camping   179
6. South Inland Camping   193

SECTION 2: ADDITIONAL STATE AND FEDERAL CAMPGROUNDS

7. U.S. Army Corps of Engineers Sites   219
8. Bureau of Land Management Sites   223
9. California State Forests   229

10. California State Parks   233
11. National Parks   263
12. U.S. Forest Service Sites   269

Index   289

ACKNOWLEDGMENTS

I could never have completed this book without the knowledge, help, and cooperation of hundreds of people. Among these were dozens of park rangers who shared their expertise in evaluating campgrounds; fellow campers, many whose names I never learned, who told of their recent experiences at parks I had not visited for a number of years; my wife and son, who endured my attention to work as we traveled around the state camping; and the staff of Prima Publishing, who made it possible. I would like to extend my heartfelt thanks to all who knowingly and unknowingly assisted me in my research.

A very special thanks goes to Jennifer Bayse, who came up with the idea and helped me develop it.

INTRODUCTION

California is a land where families can camp in wilderness areas far from crowded cities. From the rain forests of the rugged North Coast to the stark, dry lands of the Mojave Desert; from the sagebrush-covered lava beds of the Modoc Plateau to the semitropical sandy beaches of the South Coast; from the rolling, green hills near the San Francisco Bay to the cold mountain streams and blue alpine lakes in the High Sierra, California offers a wider variety of camping opportunities than any other state in the nation. And since camping is enjoyed year-round in California, it's the perfect family activity.

Camping brings out the pioneer in us all. Isolated campgrounds where children can experience the quiet wilderness—and where they can gain a sense of independence and adventure as they explore—give them and their whole family a break from the hectic pace of everyday life.

This guide provides ideas for family outings that enhance family camaraderie and encourage the outdoor activities many families never experience, such as waking to the sounds of chicory squirrels scolding invaders as the sun filters through tall fir and pine trees, scarfing down a hearty breakfast cooked over a campfire, spending a day along a trail or stream where unexpected adventures lurk, or just snoozing on a sleeping pad in the warmth of a summer afternoon. All these activities make family camping one of the most fulfilling, least expensive outings available.

If you are an experienced camper, the following sections will confirm what you have learned by trial and error over the years, so you may want to skip directly to the campground entries. But if you are new to the world of camping, please read with care the suggestions on how to organize your outings. These pointers, from what to take along to wear and eat, to how to keep warm at night, will help make your outings more enjoyable. Although camping is an inherently enjoyable activity—and it is difficult to make a camping trip to a good campground a bad experience—the simple guidelines that follow will make it easy to enjoy unforgettable trips almost every time you camp.

TIPS FOR CAMPING WITH KIDS

When adults camp there is always a margin of error where a few mistakes only make the outing more memorable. When families with young children camp, that margin of error is much smaller, and the consequences of mistakes can be severe. Mistakes that would pose only a small problem for adults can lead to a catastrophe when small children are involved.

A chance drenching without a change of clothes may make an adult cold and uncomfortable, but the same experience could make a small child—and everyone around him or her—miserable. It could also lead to hypothermia. A night slightly colder than expected will make adults shiver as they huddle under whatever extra covers can be found, but the same chill will keep a small child awake all night, along with everyone else.

It is easy to avoid these and other pitfalls, however, and the following suggestions will help those new to camping with children do just that.

WHERE TO GO

Outdoor travel writer Tom Stienstra has said that 95 percent of vacationers in California use 5 percent of the available recreation areas. The other 5 percent head for hidden jewels where they enjoy spectacular scenery with few crowds. Many novice campers, especially those with young children, are reluctant to head to out-of-the-way sites where facilities are few and distances to services are far. More experienced campers head for just those campgrounds for the solitude found there. The campgrounds in this guide include samples of both types of camping.

As you read through the entries that follow in Section 1, you will find one for Yosemite National Park where the campgrounds are overflowing most of the year with thousands of campers crowded into densely packed sites. You will also find another for Lava Beds National Monument, where the solitary campground sits among thousands of acres of desolate wilderness where few others roam.

It's up to you where you head on your camping excursions, but the information in this guide will help you choose outings where everyone in the family can enjoy a fun-filled vacation that will become part of the family lore. Oh, there will be some trips that will stick in your family's collective mind because of mishaps (someone fell in a cold creek and had to spend the rest of the day wrapped in a blanket inside the tent because all his or her other clothes were already wet) and because of mistakes (someone forgot to pack mustard and catsup for the hotdogs or spilled all the popcorn in the campfire). These memories of mistake-filled trips, though, only serve to make the memory of those trips where everything fell into place even more pleasant.

Before you make plans for a trip, have the whole family look over the entries for the region where you plan to head, noting what is offered nearby for everyone in the family. Is there a place where the toddler can play safely with minimal supervision? What about something to interest even recalcitrant teens who want to take CD players, curling irons, and other necessities of modern life along as they head for the untamed wilderness? Don't neglect your needs, either. Is there something for you in the mix?

After you have made a tentative decision, give the park or forest service ranger a call to make sure the activities described in the entry are still current. Sometimes trails get washed out, campfire programs canceled, or even whole campgrounds closed. If all is as mentioned in the guide, then go ahead with your plans.

WHAT TO TAKE

It is easy to load down your vehicle with so much equipment and food that there isn't room for the family to ride in comfort. How do you decide what is really necessary and what is just so much extra baggage? It isn't always easy. First, consider what weather is likely to occur during your trip. If there is almost no possibility of it being cold and wet, then leave heavy coats and space-consuming rain gear home. If you know that fogs will dampen the vegetation each night, then take a roomy tent where everyone can escape the dripping mist. Use the checklist that follows to help you decide what you will need for each outing and what you will want to leave home.

You certainly will want to bring along a tent or tents where the whole family can sleep comfortably out of the rain and wind that may come up in the night. And warm bedding is a must for an enjoyable trip. Check the temperature rating of your sleeping bags, and take extra blankets if you are heading for a campground where the nightly temperatures even occasionally fall below what your bags are rated.

You also need to take plenty of layered clothing, including rain gear, for everyone. With layers you can feel comfortable in early morning chill and afternoon heat. Don't worry about changing dirty clothes on the trip, but make sure you have several changes in case someone gets wet. My wife and I once spent a week at Patrick's Point State Park along the North Coast with our ten-year-old son and the clothes he got wet on the first day were still damp when we left five days later. We were forever thankful that we had overpacked for him. We couldn't have stayed for the week without heading for the local Laundromat if we hadn't, and some camp-grounds don't have a Laundromat nearby.

Flashlights and lanterns are also a necessity. They don't have to be large or expensive, but just powerful enough to help you find your way around after dark. Some families like to make their campsite as bright as their living room, but I always find such powerful lights distracting when I camp. I prefer more subdued lighting where the shadows can invade the camp and add a feeling of suspense and adventure.

Among the objects you don't want to burden yourself with are too many toys, especially bulky ones. While your children may feel they can't live for a week without the current toy craze, take only a few small items for those quiet times when no one wants to leave camp. The children can then play quietly with their toys while the adults laze around beneath the shade of tall trees.

One large item you may want to consider taking along, however, is a bicycle. Most campgrounds have lightly trav-eled roads where children can ride safely, and many trails are appropriate for off-road biking. Children can spend energetic time riding their bikes while you enjoy a few moments of silence.

FOOD FOR THE WHOLE FAMILY

This is one area where novice campers have some difficulty. How do you plan menus for a trip where you won't have the opportunity to pop down to the corner grocery store for those items that you forgot? The key is to select easily pre-pared meals that can be cooked on a two-burner camp stove and that require only nonperishable ingredients.

While you may not use prepared meals regularly at home, they come in handy on campouts because they take up less packing space than meals with many fresh ingredients and generally require fewer pots and pans to prepare. In addi-tion, children generally like the taste of them. If you do bring along fresh meats and vegetables, make sure they are kept cool, then cooked thoroughly.

Make sure your meal selections meet everyone's approval and don't forget desserts and snacks, both for after dinner when S'Mores, popcorn, and hot chocolate are greatly enjoyed, and for the afternoon when exercise makes the whole family hungry.

FISHING, HIKING, AND OTHER RECREATIONAL ACTIVITIES
Some of the most enjoyable moments of camping come when the family leaves the luxuries and recreational tools of home behind and heads out into the wilderness on hiking or fishing trips. These require little in the way of equipment (you can fish with nothing more than a piece of fishing line, a hook, and a limb off a willow or alder), and all ages can get into the activity without a lot of preparation.

Some prefer to use more modern fishing equipment, but it isn't necessary to spend lots of money to purchase perfectly adequate rods and reels that will give years of service. Sporting goods, fishing, and outdoor equipment stores all sell plenty of inexpensive gear and are willing to help novices make their selections.

Special shoes and boots are really not necessary for most light hiking done on camping trips, but you should take along a canteen of water and a small day pack for carrying snacks. A pair of binoculars, maybe a magnifying glass, and a map of the trails around the campground are the only other items you may want to pack for hiking trips.

If your family enjoys a special activity such as birding or collecting rocks, you can always bring along a few field guides to help with identification along the trail. Remember, however, that collecting any natural object is prohibited in state and national parks, and may be restricted in some areas of the national forests.

Adopting the phrase "take nothing but pictures, leave nothing but footprints" as your motto is an excellent way to ensure that those who follow you into a natural area will have as much to view as you did.

HEALTH AND SAFETY

Safety is always an issue when venturing into the outdoors, but over the years my family has experienced no more injuries when camping than when we were at home. The most significant safety factor on camping trips is the danger of children getting lost. While there is no way to guarantee that your children will not wander away from the campground and get lost, you can prepare them for the possibility.

First, train them to always let you know what direction they are heading in when they do leave the campsite. Second, prepare them for what they must do if they become lost. For example, give children a whistle to carry at all times when camping. If they feel they are lost, train them to stop, hug a tree (or a bush or a stone), and blow the whistle as loudly as possible. If they have not wandered too far off the maintained trails, someone is very likely to hear the whistle. Make sure they know not to panic and to stay in one spot if the first whistles don't bring help. Finally, tell them to wait calmly for help to come to them. Help will come, even if they are far from the trails; camp rangers are trained to search for lost children.

Health issues aren't a major concern while camping, but your family should follow several common hygiene practices while preparing food. Keep your hands washed when you are preparing meals, keep perishables cool, cook all meats and poultry thoroughly, and clean up after all meals.

If you're going to camp in a national forest, you need to know that many of the smaller campgrounds have sparse facilities and few have piped water. It is advisable to check with the local ranger about what facilities are available in the campgrounds.

Most of the untreated waters of California are infected with *Giardia,* a bacterium that can cause stomach cramps and diarrhea. If you draw water from a source that you suspect is not potable, such as from a lake or stream, be sure to purify the water before consuming it. Use either a commercial filtration unit or boil the water for ten minutes.

Always pack a first aid kit for the scrapes, cuts, and bruises that can occur while camping. These are no worse in the outdoors than at home, but you should be a little more careful about cleaning out the wounds and covering them tightly to keep out any bacteria that may be lurking in the soil.

Two first aid items that you should never leave home without are adequate supplies of sunscreen and insect repellent. With these two protectants, everyone will be much more comfortable under the summer sun and during nights full of hungry mosquitos.

As a last note, don't forget to bring any prescription medicine someone in the family may be taking. A campsite in the wilderness is not the place to discover you've forgotten to bring along the antihistamines the children take for their allergies, or any other prescription.

WILDLIFE ENCOUNTERS

One of the main reasons for camping is to experience wilderness and to enjoy the many things about undeveloped areas that are lost in our modern world. Although most parents would agree with this, many also have fears about too much wildness. What happens if we encounter a mountain lion as we walk along a trail? What if my child finds a rattlesnake? And what about bears? These are all questions that spring to parents' minds as they camp in an area for the first time, and they are all legitimate.

Just because they are legitimate questions, though, doesn't mean that you have to be afraid of the natural world. Taking a few basic precautions in the natural world will almost, although I must admit not completely, guarantee a safe outing.

Rattlesnakes abound in the wild throughout California. They live in hot areas, in open country, among rocky outcroppings, and near waterways—all places where families head to camp. This will surprise many campers, for they have camped for years without ever seeing a rattlesnake. And they may camp for many more without encountering one.

Rattlesnakes are reclusive characters that are more terrified of humans than humans are of them. They only attack large mammals when they are afraid and have no escape.

For us, that means you can avoid them, even in parks and campgrounds where they are abundant, by teaching everyone to take several easy precautions. One, always look before placing your hands or feet in hidden crevices where the snakes may be sleeping. Two, never rush into rocky or grassy areas. Always take it slowly and make plenty of noise to give the snakes an opportunity to slink away. Three, be aware of your surroundings, and watch for all wildlife that may live in the area. That way you will see any rattlesnakes around and not come upon them unexpectedly.

Mountain lions have been in the news in recent years as humans have invaded their habitats in larger and larger numbers. Although lion attacks have occurred, and one death has been attributed to such an attack, these are infrequent. Again, mountain lions are generally reclusive animals that do not like to encounter humans. I have hiked and explored the wildlands of California for almost forty years, and have seen only two lions. And one of those was along a stream as I was driving down the highway.

Precautions recommended if you do encounter a lion on the trail are to stand tall, wave your arms, pick any young children up on your shoulders, and don't run. In other words, make yourself seem as large as possible to the lion. In regions where there have been a number of sightings this also means you should not let young children wander along backcountry trails alone.

Bears are another large mammal that you may encounter in campgrounds. In general, they are even less of a threat to humans than rattlesnakes and mountain lions. You are only really endangered when you come between a mother and her cubs or interfere with a bear that is eating.

My teenage son and I had an encounter with a bear on a recent backpacking trip when we awoke to the sounds of our food bag being ripped open. Although we had hung it on a limb, we didn't choose one small enough to keep a two-year-old bear from climbing out for it.

We were within fifteen feet of this young bear for over an hour as he gorged himself on our food supply, yet he never threatened us in any way. He would have, however, if either of us had been foolish enough to challenge him around the food. He also might have attacked us if we had attempted to run away from him.

As with mountain lions, don't run, and teach your children not to run, if you encounter a bear. With bears, though, you don't want to make threatening moves or make yourself larger the way you do with lion. Simply stay still, or slowly back away, and keep from attracting too much attention as you leave the area.

Probably more of a threat to you and your children are the small furry animals that scurry around almost every campground in California. These are the ground squirrels and chipmunks that feed on the leftovers of previous campers. Although they may look harmless, both are carriers of bubonic plague and rabies. Avoid handling them or letting your children feed them. They are best watched from a distance.

EQUIPMENT AND SUPPLIES CHECKLIST

Since each family will have its own special needs, I have not attempted to make this a comprehensive checklist. Rather, I have made a list of what I consider minimal needs for the average family heading for a developed campground. I assume that those who are heading into undeveloped campgrounds and regions where they must camp without any amenities have acquired a basic understanding of what they need to survive comfortably on camping trips.

Shelter and Sleeping Supplies

Don't get too fancy here. A good tent (or tents) that provides shelter for the whole family in relative comfort during rain, wind, and blustery weather is a necessity. Sleeping bags with a temperature rating at least as low as the average low readings for the area where you are heading and a pad or air mattress for each person are the only other items you'll need for a good night's rest. This equipment should be compact and easily assembled, but that does not mean it must be expensive. Check with your local sporting goods or outdoor equipment store for advice on selecting good, inexpensive equipment that will meet the needs of your family.

Ground covers for laying beneath the tents or for anyone sleeping outside are also a good idea, although not absolutely necessary.

- Tent
- Sleeping bags
- Pads or air mattresses
- Pillows
- Ground covers
- Flashlights for each member of your family (with extra batteries)

Clothing and Personal Gear

Again, don't go overboard. It's nice to have clean clothes for everyone, but it's more important to have adequate layers of clothing to keep everyone warm and dry in the normal weather for the region where you are heading. In addition, pack at least one replacement for each layer of clothing you carry. While this may not keep everyone in clean clothes, it will keep them warm and comfortable, even if one set of clothes gets wet.

One important item here is a hat or cap for everyone. Since many campgrounds are located at high elevations, it is important to wear a hat that will help protect your face from the sun. Hats also help keep you warm in cold, windy weather, since most heat loss occurs through the head.

While many people spend a lot of money to buy special boots for camping, this is necessary only if you plan to do extensive hiking on rugged trails where you need the ankle and sole support. Otherwise, simply take along a couple of pairs of grungy sneakers.

You should pack two of the following for each person in your family:

- Pants
- Short-sleeve shirts or T-shirts
- Long-sleeve shirts or sweatshirts
- Jackets or windbreakers (weight depends on the weather you're anticipating)
- Socks (add a few additional pairs of these since they take up little room and wet socks are a real nuisance)
- Sneakers or boots

Pack at least one of each of the following for each member of the family:

- Hat or cap
- Rain gear
- Towel and washcloth
- Assorted toiletry items such as soap, toothpaste, toothbrush, comb, and toilet paper

Cooking Accessories

This is one area where you'll have to look at your menu to determine the minimum amount of cookware to take. Pots and pans take up a lot of space, but careful planning can reduce the amount needed.

- Pots and pans (bring the minimum)
- Eating utensils (bring minimum for each person)
- Cooking stove (I suggest a two-burner propane stove)
- Extra fuel
- Lantern for lighting cook area after dark (this can also be used for reading or games after meals)
- Any special utensils needed for special meals (such as coat hangers for roasting marshmallows)
- A large water container for use around the campsite

Miscellaneous Items

Always make a list of those small items that you may need or want when you are on your trip. These can be as simple as extra film for the camera or a compass for cross-country hikes. Such a list varies for each family and for each member. Here are a few things you may want to add to your list:

- Compass
- Camera with extra film and batteries
- Pocket knife
- Car games for traveling to and from the campground
- Clothesline and clothespins for drying wet clothes
- Notebooks and pencils
- Cards for evening games
- Books for everyone to read
- Sewing kit
- Cots for those sleeping outside tents

These checklists are just ideas. You will develop your own as you camp, so take notes on what you had too much or not enough of on each trip. In this way you can refine your lists and preparations so you'll always have everything, or at least almost everything, you'll need.

RESERVATIONS

Most state parks are on the State Parks Reservation System at least part of the year. National parks and national forests also have their own reservation systems, although most national forest campgrounds are on a first-come, first-served basis.

For any state park that is on the State Parks Reservation System, the number to call is (800) 444-PARK. For any national park that is on a reservation system, the number to call is (800) 365-CAMP. For national forest campgrounds on a reservation system, the number is (800) 283-CAMP.

If you are unsure if the campground you wish to visit is

on a reservation system, call the park headquarters and they will let you know.

HOW TO
USE THIS GUIDE

T his guide has two major sections. Section 1 includes
entries for campgrounds around the state that I feel
offer exceptional places to camp with kids. These are
divided into six regions: North Coast, North Inland, Central
Coast, Central Inland, South Coast, and South Inland. Each
of these sections includes my favorite campgrounds with
complete information about the activities available there. The
entries include recommendations for the age of children who
might enjoy the area, the location of the campground, camping facilities, hiking activities, and special outings and activities in or near the campground.

Section 2 is a comprehensive listing of state and federal
lands where you can camp, if you like less popular places
where you can explore California's natural wonders on your
own. Less information is given about the camping facilities,
but a contact number is provided if you to wish investigate
an area further.

If you are a novice camper, begin your search for a campground in Section 1 and gain some knowledge of the various
regions of California before heading to less visited and less
known areas. If you're an experienced camper, you may want
to head straight for Section 2 to discover new camping areas.

OUTSTANDING CAMPGROUNDS FOR KIDS

CHAPTER 1

NORTH COAST CAMPING

You'll encounter giants as you travel along California's North Coast. Not Paul Bunyan-type giants, but giant sequoia, better known as coastal redwoods. These forest behemoths reach heights of 300 feet and flourish along a narrow stretch of land from Santa Cruz north to the Oregon border.

Wet winters and foggy summers provide the forests with the moisture needed to nourish the tall trees and lush understory, and water from heavy winter rains feeds the many streams and rivers that cut through the rugged mountains and steep canyons of the coastal range. These streams and rivers in turn become the habitat for migrating salmon and steelhead trout, who head upstream to spawning grounds.

The parks and national forests in this region offer excellent recreational opportunities in lush forests, along streams and rivers, and on long, wild beaches.

Rare and endangered birds such as the northern spotted owl and marbled murrelet use the remaining old-growth forests of the region for nesting sites, and large Roosevelt elk roam meadows and canyons of several state parks.

Summer is the best time to take family camping trips in the region, for the winters are just too wet: over 100 inches

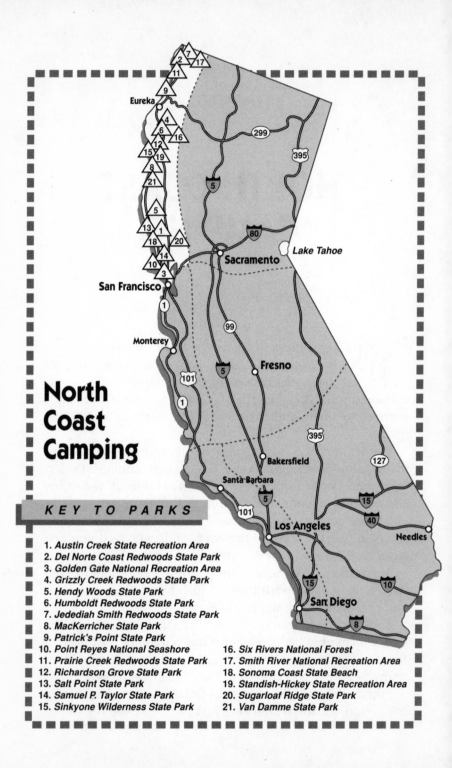

North Coast Camping

KEY TO PARKS

1. *Austin Creek State Recreation Area*
2. *Del Norte Coast Redwoods State Park*
3. *Golden Gate National Recreation Area*
4. *Grizzly Creek Redwoods State Park*
5. *Hendy Woods State Park*
6. *Humboldt Redwoods State Park*
7. *Jedediah Smith Redwoods State Park*
8. *MacKerricher State Park*
9. *Patrick's Point State Park*
10. *Point Reyes National Seashore*
11. *Prairie Creek Redwoods State Park*
12. *Richardson Grove State Park*
13. *Salt Point State Park*
14. *Samuel P. Taylor State Park*
15. *Sinkyone Wilderness State Park*
16. *Six Rivers National Forest*
17. *Smith River National Recreation Area*
18. *Sonoma Coast State Beach*
19. *Standish-Hickey State Recreation Area*
20. *Sugarloaf Ridge State Park*
21. *Van Damme State Park*

of rain falls between November and March in some areas. Even the drier spots exceed 60 inches a year.

Even though little rain falls in the summer along the North Coast, fog shrouds areas near the ocean until well past noon on most days. My family and I once camped for over a week at Patrick's Point State Park north of Trinidad. Clothes that had gotten wet on our first day there were still too wet to store when we left.

It's imperative that you take plenty of clothes and good rain gear when you head for the North Coast. With plenty of rain gear, warm clothes, and a good tent, however, your family can enjoy great camping adventures in this section of California.

AUSTIN CREEK STATE RECREATION AREA
17000 Armstrong Woods Road
Guerneville, CA 95446
(707) 869-2015

This wild and isolated recreation area lies in rugged, oak-covered hills in the mountainous terrain above Armstrong Redwoods State Preserve, not far from the mouth of the Russian River in Sonoma County, about two hours north of San Francisco. Over twenty miles of trails lead beneath oak forests, through open grassland, and along year-round creeks. Panoramic views display distant ridges, and wild azaleas bloom along the creeks during late spring.

The elevations within the 4,236-acre area range from 150 feet along the lower reaches of Austin Creek to 1,940 feet at the top of McCray Mountain.

Recommended Ages
Poor for toddlers and preschoolers, Good for 6–9, Best for 10 and over.

Location
The recreation area is near Guerneville on the Russian River.

Take California 116 off U.S. 101 at Cotati about fifty miles north of the Golden Gate Bridge and head west to Guerneville. In Guerneville take Armstrong Woods Road north for three miles to the entrance to Armstrong Redwoods State Preserve. The recreation area is located on the ridges behind the preserve.

Camping Facilities

A twenty-four-site campground sits alongside the shores of Bullfrog Pond on the ridge above Armstrong Grove. All sites have tables, stove pits, and food lockers. Piped water and bathrooms are nearby. No trailers, or campers/motor homes over twenty feet, are accommodated because of the narrow, winding access road.

Three primitive trail camps are located along Gilliam and Austin creeks. All campsites are open year-round except for occasional closures during times of high fire danger. The sites are available on a first-come, first-served basis.

Of the hike-in campsites I prefer the most distant one, Mannings Flat Trail Camp, along East Austin Creek. The site is spectacular, situated among the oak trees that line the creek, and few people hike in the three-plus miles to the site.

Hiking Activities

There are over twenty miles of trails in the recreation area that lead down to the dark redwood forests of Armstrong Grove and to open grasslands dotted with oak in the recreation area.

A service road leads less than a mile to the top of McCray Mountain, the highest point in the recreation area at 1,940 feet.

A four-mile loop leads from the campground, down East Ridge Trail into the redwoods, to the Pool Ridge Trail, and back up the ridge to the campground. This is an excellent day hike, and it can be broken up with a picnic in the redwoods.

A service road leads from the campground a mile down a steep grade to Gilliam Creek. Gilliam Creek Trail leads off from that and follows the creek downhill past several seasonal waterfalls and to summer swimming holes. The Gilliam Creek Trail Camp is a little over two miles from Bullfrog Pond, and a service road leads along East Austin Creek for a mile to the East Austin Creek Trail. From that junction you can head back uphill for a little over two miles to the campground.

Several other good trails lead along creeks where the kids can fish, play in the water, or explore for small aquatic plants and animals.

The hills are covered with thick blooms of wildflowers in the late spring, and shaded spots along the creeks have large groves of wild azalea. Many times you can smell these fragrant bushes before you see them.

Special Outings and Activities

In the summer the exposed hillsides in the recreation area can be hot, and old and young alike appreciate a dip in cool water. The best spots for these activities are in the deep holes along East Austin and Gilliam creeks. The shore of Bullfrog Pond is filled with rushes and cattails, making even wading difficult. Youngsters like to try their luck at fishing in the pond, and an occasional bluegill does take the bait.

Horse trail rides are available through a concessionaire in Armstrong Grove. Both half- or full-day rides are offered.

If you wish to explore among the tall redwoods but don't want to make the long trek back uphill, you can drive down to the picnic area and walk along the level pathways that lead to the more outstanding trees.

DEL NORTE COAST REDWOODS STATE PARK
4241 Kings Valley Road
Crescent City, CA 95531
(707) 464-9533

This state redwoods park is a temperate rain forest with an average annual rainfall of 110 inches. The dense redwood forests within the 6,375-acre park grow down to the ocean's edge, and many of the groves are virgin growth.

Over twenty miles of hiking trails lead through the forests on the east side of U.S. 101, and several more miles of trail lead to the ocean on the west side of the highway.

Recommended Ages
Good for toddlers and preschoolers, Excellent for 6–9 and for 10 and over.

Location
The park includes virgin groves of redwoods on both sides of U.S. 101 about seven miles south of Crescent City.

Camping Facilities
Two campgrounds, Casara and Red Alder, with a total of 145 developed campsites, sit on the site of a 1920s logging operation. Showers and restrooms are located throughout the campgrounds.

Trailers to twenty-seven feet and camper/motor homes to thirty-one feet are accommodated.

The park and campgrounds are open from April through October each year, and the campgrounds are on the State Park Reservation System May through September.

Hiking Activities
A short nature loop trail leads out from the entrance station and introduces hikers to the natural history of the park. Alder Basin Loop Trail encircles the Casara Campground, and the Trestle Loop Trail the Red Alder Campground.

Longer trails include the Mill Creek, Saddler Skyline, and Hobbs Wall trails. These all lead from the campground into the depths of lush stands of virgin redwoods, and Mill Creek Trail leads along a beautiful year-round creek where children can fish, wade in shallow pools, and even swim in the cool waters of deeper pools on the occasional warm day during midsummer.

Although none of the trails that begin from the camp-

The treeless landscape of the Marin Headlands features
excellent hiking into environmental campgrounds of the
Golden Gate National Recreation Area.

grounds lead to the ocean on the west side of U.S. 101, there
are several trailheads off U.S. 101 about five miles south of
the park entrance that lead to backpack campsites along the
ocean in Redwood National Park adjacent to the state park.
These trails make good day hikes for older children.

Special Outings and Activities
This park caters to families with children and provides struc-
tured activities for a wide age span. There are natural history

exhibits at the information center, guided walks led by rangers are offered during the day for several age groups, a Junior Ranger program gets youth involved in the daily operation of the park, and campfires are held almost every night during the summer.

Come prepared for cold, damp weather even during the summer. The campgrounds are located in the fog belt of the North Coast, and the huge redwoods block out most of the sun even during midday.

Throughout the year the Redwood National and State Parks Field Seminars holds occasional events and classes at Del Norte and other parks in the redwood region. Check with the Events Coordinator, Redwood National and State Parks Field Seminars, 1111 Second Street, Crescent City, CA 95531; (707) 465-4113, for a catalog of current offerings. Many of these classes fill early, so send for a catalog as soon as you know you are going to be in the region to ensure a spot in the class of your choice. Many of the classes are for kids or the whole family.

GOLDEN GATE NATIONAL RECREATION AREA
Fort Mason
San Francisco, CA 94123
(415) 556-0560

This large recreation area is the most visited unit of the National Park Service with some 20 million visitors a year. Although portions of the area are located in urban settings in San Francisco, most of it is located in undeveloped regions of Marin County to the north of the Golden Gate. The more than 27,000 acres of open grasslands and redwood forests of the Marin Headlands and Mt. Tamalpais are crisscrossed with excellent hiking trails. Several of these lead to the only campsites within the recreation area.

These hike-in camps are great introductions to backpacking for children of all ages, and their close proximity to the large population of the San Francisco Bay Region makes them popular with families.

Recommended Ages
Poor for toddlers and preschoolers, Good for 6–9, Excellent for 10 and over.

Location
The hike-in campgrounds are located to the west of U.S. 101 just north of the Golden Gate Bridge.

Camping Facilities
There are no drive-in campgrounds in the recreation area, but the three hike-in campgrounds offer families with younger, inexperienced backpackers a chance to take overnight hikes with a minimum of worry and trouble.

The easiest of these is Bicentennial Camp near Point Bonita, where you have less than a quarter-mile hike into three sites that accommodate four people each. These sites have a chemical toilet, picnic tables, and grills, but no water.

Haypress Camp is three-quarters of a mile from the parking area, and has six sites that each hold four people. These also have a chemical toilet and picnic tables, but no water. Open fires are not allowed.

Hawk Camp is four miles from parking and has three sites for four people each. This site also has chemical toilets and tables, but no water. Open fires are not allowed.

These campsites are open year-round, and reservations are required. There is a three-day limit at each. Reservations can be made by calling the recreation area headquarters.

Hiking Activities
Hiking is required to reach all these sites, and there are also miles of adjoining trails that lead over the grass covered hills of the Marin Headlands. During the spring the hills have extravagant wildflower displays and during the fall migrating raptors fly overhead in large numbers.

Below Hawk Camp lies Gerbode Valley, a wildlife refuge where you can see a wide variety of animals, including bobcats, as you hike the trails above it.

Special Outings and Activities
You may want to head for the Marin Headlands Visitor Center at Fort Cronkhite near Rodeo Lagoon and Beach to learn about the natural history of the region before heading out on the trail. The California Marin Mammal Center is also located near Fort Cronkhite, and the whole family can learn about how sick or injured marine mammals such as harbor seals and sea lions are nursed back to health before being returned to the wild.

At the visitor center kids can checkout Discovery Packs, with bug boxes, binoculars, pocket microscopes, and dip nets, to help them explore the natural world of the headlands.

GRIZZLY CREEK REDWOODS STATE PARK
1649 Highway 36
Carlotta, CA 95528
(707) 777-3683

This 390-acre park sits on the banks of the Van Duzen River about thirty miles inland from the ocean. Grizzly Creek meanders through a grove of redwoods in the park on its way to the river. Relatively few people come to this out-of-the-way setting, but those who do enjoy the intimate park.

Recommended Ages
Good for toddlers and preschoolers, Excellent for 6–9 and for 10 and over.

Location
The park is located eighteen miles east of U.S. 101 on State Route 36 in Humboldt County.

Camping Facilities
Thirty developed campsites sit beside the Van Duzen River. Showers, restrooms, and water are scattered throughout the campground.

Sites will handle trailers to twenty-four feet and camper/

motor homes to thirty feet.

The campground is open year-round and on the State Park Reservation System from May through September.

About three miles west of the campgrounds on State Route 36 there are six environmental, walk-in campsites at Cheatham Grove.

Hiking Activities

Trails lead along Grizzly Creek, through redwood groves, and along the Van Duzen River. These are relatively flat with few climbs, and most are easily traveled by preschoolers. Just under five miles of trails traverse the park and include a marked, self-guiding nature trail across State Route 36 from the campground.

Special Outings and Activities

The park is small at 234 acres, but that gives it an intimate feeling. There is plenty of room for families to roam, and most children, from toddlers to teens, enjoy spending time along the river during midsummer, when the flow is gentle and slow moving. Toddlers enjoy wading along the edges of shallow pools, while older children search out deeper holes where they can swim and dive in the cool waters.

Fishing is a popular activity for adults in the late fall and winter, but children like to try their luck during slow summer days when little is moving along the banks of Van Duzen River and Grizzly Creek.

The park offers a full range of activities for children during the day. Rangers lead daily hikes into the redwood groves where they help children and adults explore the natural world. Children can also join in Junior Ranger and Litter-Gitter activities, where they learn about the operations of the park as well as help clean it up.

Most nights there are ranger-led campfires where visitors can learn about the history and ecology of the region.

This is another North Coast park where the Redwood National and State Parks Field Seminars holds occasional events and classes throughout the year. Check with the Events Coordinator, Redwood National and State Parks Field Seminars, 1111 Second Street, Crescent City, CA 95531; (707) 465-4113, for a catalog of current offerings.

HENDY WOODS STATE PARK
P.O. Box 440
Mendocino, CA 95460
(707) 937-5804

Two virgin groves of redwoods (the 80-acre Big Hendy and the 20-acre Little Hendy groves) and the Navarro River are the prime features of this 765-acre state park.

Families enjoy wading, fishing, swimming, and canoeing along the river, and hiking through the redwood groves.

Recommended Ages
Good for toddlers and preschoolers, Excellent for 6–9 and for 10 and over.

Location
The park sits to the south of State Route 128, some eight miles northwest of Boonville in Anderson Valley.

Camping Facilities
Two campgrounds (Azalea and Wildcat) with a total of ninety-two developed campsites are located in the middle of the park. These have showers and water, and can accommodate thirty-five-foot trailers and camper/motor homes.

The campgrounds are open year-round and are on a first-come, first-served basis during the off-season, but from mid-May through September they are on the State Park Reservation System.

Hiking Activities
Marked hiking trails are limited within Hendy Woods. Two short nature trails lead through the eighty-acre Big Hendy Grove. One is a half-mile-long self-guided discovery trail and

the other is a quarter-mile-long, wheelchair-accessible, paved path.

Another several miles of trails connect Big Hendy and Little Hendy groves with Azalea and Wildcat campgrounds.

Special Outings and Activities

The Navarro River runs along the edge of the park, and during the summer months it is a quiet, slow-moving stream with several access points. These range from shallow streams where even toddlers can explore and play in the cool waters during hot days to deeper pools where older children can dive and swim.

Many families bring inner tubes and tube down the river to a spot below the Greenwood Road bridge near the park entrance. Here they can take their tubes out of the river onto a sandy beach and walk back to camp.

During late winter and spring the water levels in the river are higher, and canoers and kayakers enjoy the faster currents.

From Memorial Day to Labor Day the park operates several programs of interest to families. During the day youth can join the Junior Ranger program as they participate in hikes and other activities where they learn about the natural history of the region. Other ranger-led hikes offer learning activities and hikes for both adults and children. Campfire programs are held on most nights during the busy season.

Fishing in the river is best from fall to spring but children like to try their luck anytime. They can also hunt for frogs and other aquatic life along the shore of the slow-moving water during the summer.

For families with horses there is a 3.3-mile-long horse trail that leads upstream along the Navarro from the rear of the park. There are no horse rental facilities nearby.

HUMBOLDT REDWOODS STATE PARK
P.O. Box 100
Weott, CA 95571
(707) 946-2409

The spectacular Avenue of the Giants runs thirty-three miles through this 51,143-acre redwood park in Humboldt County south of Eureka.

There are 247 developed campsites within the park at three campgrounds, and more than 100 miles of hiking trails that lead through virgin groves of redwoods. Several creeks wind through the park, and the elevation ranges from 150 feet at park headquarters to 3,379 feet atop Grasshopper Peak.

Recommended Ages
Good for toddlers and preschoolers, Excellent for 6–9 and for 10 and over.

Location
The park is located along U.S. 101, forty-five miles south of Eureka.

Camping Facilities
This park has the most extensive camping facilities of any state park in California. Burlington Campground, with 58 sites, is open year-round and on the State Park Reservation System from mid-April to September. Hidden Springs Campground, with 155 sites, and Albee Creek Campground, with 34 sites, are open and on the State Park Reservation System from mid-May to mid-September. They are closed the rest of the year.

These campgrounds accept trailers to twenty-four feet and camper/motor homes to thirty feet.

In addition to the above car campsites the park has six trail camps and five environmental campsites where you have to walk in to camp.

Burlington Campground is located near the park headquarters and visitor center off U.S. 101 just south of the company town of Weott. Hidden Springs is a little farther off U.S. 101 than Burlington, but still readily accessible. My favorite campground is Albee Creek, however, because it is farther from the highway and closer to trails that lead into the vir-

gin redwood groves and to trail camps where you can head
for overnight trips. I like to hike to Grasshopper Trail Camp
near the fire lookout tower on Grasshopper Peak, the highest point in the park, when I take overnight trips.

Permits are required for the trail camps and are available
at the park headquarters.

All three of the campgrounds sit beside good-size streams
or the Eel River where everyone from toddlers to teens can
enjoy the shallow ripples and deep pools during warm summer days. Children also like to fish in the deeper pools and
watch for the runs of silver and king salmon and steelhead
after the rains begin in the late fall.

Hiking Activities

The abundance of trails in the park ensure great hikes for
everyone. Hidden Springs Campground sits along the
Avenue of the Giants (U.S. 101) and a trail (two-plus miles
long) leads from it along the Eel River through the famous
Garden Club of America Grove of virgin redwoods to Burlington Campground. This is a great introductory hike on which
to learn redwood ecology, and even preschoolers enjoy it.

For those who want to explore the high country of the park,
one trail to Grasshopper Peak leads uphill from the Garden
Club of America Trail between Canoe and Feese creeks. This
five-mile round trip is strenuous and I would be reluctant to
take any but the most adventuresome children below the ages
of eight or nine on it. Another trail leads from the Albee Creek
Campground in the interior of the park.

Special Outings and Activities

The many streams that flow through the park into the Eel River
offer good fishing for families, and on warm summer days
everyone can find a good swimming hole. Toddlers and other
nonswimmers enjoy playing in shallow pools where minnows
and other small aquatic animals can be found, while swimmers search for the deeper pools where they can dive into the
clear waters from huge boulders that rise from the river.

The visitor center has exhibits, and several nature trails in the park offer a guide to plants and animals found along longer trails within the park. Rangers lead hikes for the whole family during the day, and give talks and slide shows at camp-fires at night. Children can join the Junior Ranger programs during the day, giving parents a break.

Throughout the year the Redwood National and State Parks Field Seminars holds many events and classes at Humboldt Redwoods State Park. Check with the Events Coordinator, Redwood National and State Parks Field Seminars, 1111 Second Street, Crescent City, CA 95531; (707) 465-4113, for a catalog of current offerings. The classes at this park are extremely popular and fill quickly as they are announced.

JEDEDIAH SMITH REDWOODS STATE PARK
4241 Kings Valley Road
Crescent City, CA 95531
(707) 464-9533

This is the northernmost redwoods park in California, and it lies along the banks of the largest undammed river in California, the Smith. The park terrain is level to rugged, and many trails lead from the campgrounds into groves of redwoods that rise to 340 feet with diameters to 20 feet at the base.

Recommended Ages
Excellent for all ages.

Location
The park is located on U.S. 199, nine miles northeast of Crescent City.

Camping Facilities
The 108-site campground lies between U.S. 199 and the Smith River. This developed campground accommodates thirty-foot trailers and motor homes; the tent sites all have tables, food lockers, and stove pits. Piped water and restrooms with showers are scattered throughout the campground.

I like to get a campsite in the rear of the campground near the river. This makes hiking across the summer footbridge to the trails to the interior of the park easy.

The campground is open all year and on the State Park Reservation System from mid-May through mid-September.

Hiking Activities

Several self-guided nature trails are located within the campground, and the River Trail leads from the campground to the picnic area. The most popular trails, and ones that everyone in the family from toddlers to adults can enjoy, are those that lead to the eighteen memorial groves of redwoods that have been designated within the park.

For a hike that will stretch your legs and make for a good full day outing, I like to take the Mill Creek Trail that begins across the summer footbridge from the campground. This beautiful trail leads upstream along Mill Creek across from the Howland Hill Road. After crossing Howland Hill Road the trail joins with the Boy Scout Tree Trail and continues uphill past the Boy Scout Tree to its end at Fern Falls. This is a good place to take a midday break and eat lunch before heading back to the campground.

Special Outings and Activities

Fishing in the Smith River is a popular activity for kids year-round, but adults find fly fishing for trout best between late August and the beginning of the rainy season. Salmon and steelhead migrate upstream between October and February, when fishing is generally good to excellent.

During hot summer afternoons the whole family can find a place to swim, wade, or play in shallow spots in the river or in Mill Creek, which joins the river near the campground.

Campfire talks are given at the campfire center nightly during the summer, and rangers lead walks for both kids and adults during most days.

Before heading out on hikes, either alone or with a ranger, you should visit the visitor center near the campfire center where you can learn about the ecology of the region. For even more information about the redwood region, cross the highway and head south for a short distance to the Redwood National Park Visitor Center.

The Redwood National and State Parks Field Seminars offers many classes at Jedediah Smith during the spring and summer. Check with the Events Coordinator, Redwood National and State Parks Field Seminars, 1111 Second Street, Crescent City, CA 95531; (707) 465-4113, for a catalog of current offerings.

MacKERRICHER STATE PARK
P.O. Box 440
Mendocino, CA 95460
(707) 937-5804

Beaches, bluffs, headlands, and dunes. You name an oceanside habitat and you can find it at MacKerricher. The 1,598 acres in the park include six miles of beach, Cleone Lake, and large dunes at the northern end of the park.

Hiking, bicycling, and fishing are all popular in the park, and some of the best whale-watching sites along the California coast are found on its headlands.

Recommended Ages
Excellent for all ages.

Location
The park lies along the ocean three miles north of Fort Bragg on State Route 1.

Camping Facilities
There are two campgrounds with 143 developed sites at this coastal park. Pinewood and Surfwood campgrounds are located on opposite sides of Lake Cleone, a freshwater lagoon that lies between State Route 1 and Haul Road, which runs parallel to the six-mile-long beach.

The sites accommodate thirty-five-foot trailers and motor

homes. Showers, water, and restrooms are located throughout the campgrounds. A trail leads from both campgrounds to a central campfire center where rangers lead nightly campfire talks in the summer. Surfwood is a smaller campground away from the park offices and campfire centers, and is quieter.

The campgrounds are open throughout the year and on the State Park Reservation System from April through mid-October.

Hiking Activities
The main hiking in this park is along the six miles of beach that extend from Laguna Point on the south to Ten-Mile River on the north. The hike to the seal-watching station on Laguna Point is easy for everyone from toddlers to adults, and during most of the year you can see dozens of harbor seals resting on the rocks that jut from the water just offshore.

I like to spend an easy afternoon or early evening exploring around the shore of Cleone Lake where there is abundant bird life in the rushes, reeds, and cattails in the shallow water. Many waterfowl also inhabit the shallows of the lake.

A pedestrian underpass beneath Haul Road connects the trail around Cleone Lake with the one to the seal-watching station and the beach trail.

Campers with horses are delighted to find designated equestrian trails that lead through many areas of the park, including along the beach.

Special Outings and Activities
From gray whale watching from January through March to fishing for perch both in the surf and in freshwater Cleone Lake, MacKerricher offers great opportunities for enjoying a seashore environment.

One of my favorite times to visit this wild coast is after heavy winter storms when driftwood covers large sections of the beach. Then I can search for large and small pieces of weathered wood to decorate my house and garden. If I feel particularly industrious, I build sculptures on the beach from the more esoteric pieces. These stand until the next high tide, when the structures are broken up and returned to the ocean, only to be deposited at a beach farther south.

If you have a family canoe, Lake Cleone offers safe, gentle waters for children to paddle around, and families with horses enjoy the horse trails that crisscross the park to the beach area.

During the peak season there are nightly campfire programs, and during the day rangers lead hikes for both adults and children. There is also an active Junior Ranger program for the kids.

PATRICK'S POINT STATE PARK
4150 Patrick's Point Drive
Trinidad, CA 95570
(707) 677-3570

The headlands where the park lies provide visitors with ready access to a shoreline that ranges from broad, sandy beaches to 100-foot-tall cliffs.

Although this 632-acre park is located in the heart of redwood country, there are few of these gigantic trees in the park. Instead, spruce, fir, and hemlock dominate the flat terrain of the marine terraces where the park lies.

Recommended Ages
Excellent for all ages.

Location
Patrick's Point is located twenty-five miles north of Eureka on U.S. 101 along the ocean.

Camping Facilities
Three campgrounds with 123 campsites are spread throughout the park. The campsites are secluded among tall forests of fir and spruce and almost all offer good privacy.

The sites accommodate thirty-one-foot trailers and motor

homes, and showers, bathrooms, and piped water are located throughout the campgrounds.

For access to the beach, camp at Agate Campground. Abalone and Penn campgrounds are nearer the campfire center.

This campground is excellent for bike riding, with long stretches of paved roads within the park.

The campgrounds are open year-round and on the State Park Reservation System from mid-May through mid-September.

Hiking Activities

My favorite trail in this park is the Rim Trail that leads from Agate Campground in the northern section of the park to Palmer's Point near the campfire center in the southern portion. Short trails lead from the Rim Trail to view points such as Mussel Rocks, Wedding Rock, Patrick's Point, Rocky Point, Abalone Point, and Palmer's Point. In between these sites where you can view birds and seals feeding offshore, you walk through forests of spruce, hemlock, pine, fir, and red alder.

How far you plan to hike on this trail determines what age groups will enjoy the hike. Since most of the trail is level and requires little in the way of exertion, even the very young can enjoy short stretches.

Another good trail, but one that requires a little more climbing, is the Agate Beach Trail. This trail leads from Agate Campground down a steep bluff to the beach far below. Although the trail can be steep in places, its many switchbacks make going down quite easy even for toddlers. Coming back up is a different matter, however, and parents should be prepared to carry young children at least part of the way back to the campground area.

Special Outings and Activities

Beachcombing, Junior Ranger programs, ranger-led hikes for adults and children, and fishing are the most popular activ-

Many campgrounds are located near safe beaches such as this one in Tomales Bay State Park inside Point Reyes National Seashore.

ities other than hiking in this park. There are also nightly campfire programs during the summer.

Children like to explore the reconstructed Native American village, Sumeg Village, where they can learn about how the original residents of the region lived. During the latter part of June each year the annual Sumeg Village Days are held in the village, where sacred dances, demonstrations, and celebrations commemorate the lives of the Native Americans. This event starts with healing dances that begin at dusk on a Thursday night, and various activities continue throughout the weekend.

This is a popular park for the Redwood National and State Parks Field Seminars, and many events and classes are offered here throughout the year. Check with the Events Coordinator, Redwood National and State Parks Field Seminars, 1111 Second Street, Crescent City, CA 95531; (707) 465-4113, for a catalog of current offerings. Many classes fill quickly and you should get on the mailing list if you want your choice of classes.

POINT REYES NATIONAL SEASHORE

Point Reyes, CA 94956-9799
(415) 663-1092

This 65,303-acre seashore, noted for its long beaches, tall cliffs, and lagoons, is located in the northern part of the Golden Gate National Recreation Area. The Point Reyes Peninsula is an island that has moved north from the Santa Barbara area over the past several million years and is only temporarily adjoined to Marin County. It is slowly making its way north along the west side of the San Andreas Fault.

The forests on the ridges of the peninsula and the rocks in the cliffs are unlike any others nearby and are worth exploring.

Although there is no car camping at the seashore, there are a number of backpack camps where families can take relatively easy hikes as an introduction to longer backpack trips in more isolated regions.

Recommended Ages

Poor for toddlers and preschoolers for camping, Good for 6–9, and Excellent for 10 and over.

Location

The seashore is about thirty-five miles north of San Francisco.

Camping Facilities

Only backpack camps are available at the seashore, and the four camps in the Bear Valley region of the park are Sky Camp with twelve sites, Glen Camp with twelve sites, Coast Camp with fourteen sites, and Wildcat Group Camp with three sites. The sites at the first three are limited to eight people, and those at Wildcat accommodate ten.

These camps are extremely popular and reservations are accepted up to sixty days in advance. If you wish to backpack camp at the seashore during the spring, summer, and fall, you should plan well ahead to ensure that there will be openings.

Glen Camp is the easiest hike, while Coast and Wildcat are the most difficult. With inexperienced hikers you should try for Sky or Glen, and head for Coast and Wildcat (which is limited to defined groups) with experienced ones.

The camps are open all year.

Hiking Activities

Part of the fun getting to the backpack camp is the hiking. This varies considerably from camp to camp. To reach Sky Camp you must climb about 1,000 feet in just under three miles from the Bear Valley Visitor Center. The views of Drakes Bay and the surrounding country of the Point Reyes Peninsula make the trek well worth the effort, though.

Glen Camp is a bit farther at 4.6 miles, but all of these are almost level. The camp sits in a small wooded valley about 2 miles from the ocean, and this makes day hikes from the camp easy and inviting.

Coast Camp is 6.5 miles from the trailhead at Bear Valley, but almost all of the trails leading there are level if you take the Bear Valley Trail. If you decide to take the shorter Inverness Trail you will encounter steeper trails. You have to decide if saving a half mile offsets the difference in climbs. The camp sits on an open, grassy bluff about 200 yards above the beach; the wind frequently whips off the ocean here, and there are no sheltering trees. Day hikes along the Coast Trail from the camp lead to great views of the coast.

If you camp in the park on weekends you can only stay for one night at each site, so day hikes become movement days from one camp to the next. On weekdays you can stay for two nights at each site, making short day hikes possible.

In addition to hiking to and from the backpack camps, there are dozens of other trails in the national seashore that offer great hiking. Reaching these trails entails long hikes out from the camps and then moderate drives, however, and are better left for day visits to the seashore rather than attempted as day hikes on backpack trips.

Special Outings and Activities

Special outings are almost unlimited within the national seashore, but they are generally located away from the trail camps. You can, however, watch for whales, enjoy great wildflower blooms, and keep an eye out for the exotic fallow deer that roam the hillsides as you hike to your trail camp.

Well worth staying an extra day to view are the exhibits at the visitor center and also two nearby attractions: the Earthquake Trail, where you can learn about the tectonic activity that occurred during the great 1906 quake that destroyed much of San Francisco, and the Morgan Horse Farm, where you can learn about how the National Park Service raises and trains Morgan horses for use by park rangers throughout the West.

Also nearby is a reconstructed Native American village, Kule Loklo, where you can explore buildings much like those used by the Native Americans who lived in the area for over 2,000 years before the first Europeans arrived.

Farther afield you can drive to the Pierce Ranch area where you are likely to see herds of young tule elk bulls, then continue on to the Point Reyes Lighthouse.

During the year, two major events, Pierce Ranch Day and Kule Loklo Big Time, offer families an opportunity to join in celebrations. Pierce Ranch Day takes place the first Saturday in May at the renovated Pierce Ranch in the northern section of the seashore. There visitors can explore the historic structures on the ranch as they enjoy a May Day celebration.

Kule Loklo Big Time is held in mid-June, and everyone in the family can watch traditional arts and crafts demonstrations and try his or her hand at basket making, drilling seashells, and grinding acorns.

Kids can also pick up a Junior Ranger pamphlet when they visit the visitor center. This pamphlet gives information about the naturalist activities available in the park that can lead to a Junior Ranger badge.

Point Reyes Field Seminars offers classes and seminars year-round on the natural history of the region. Many of these are designed for kids or the whole family. Contact them at

Point Reyes Field Seminars, Bear Valley Road, Point Reyes Station, CA 94956; (415) 663-1200.

PRAIRIE CREEK REDWOODS STATE PARK
Orick, CA 95555
(707) 488-2171

This 12,544-acre park has large groves of redwoods, lush fern canyons, and wild beaches. Also, the largest herd of Roosevelt elk in the state roams the meadows and bluffs of the park. The level top of an ancient marine terrace provides large flat areas where campers can explore the park, and precipitous bluffs drop to wide beaches.

Recommended Ages
Excellent for all ages.

Location
Prairie Creek lies fifty miles north of Eureka along U.S. 101.

Camping Facilities
Elk Prairie and Gold Bluffs Beach are the two developed campgrounds in this large redwood park. Elk Prairie has seventy-five developed campsites that accommodate trailers up to twenty-four feet and motor homes to twenty-seven feet. Gold Bluffs Beach lies at the end of an unpaved road and has twenty-five campsites that accommodate vehicles up to twenty feet long and seven feet wide.

There are some environmental campsites near Gold Bluffs, as well as campsites for hikers and bicyclists near both campgrounds. Both have showers scattered throughout the campground.

Elk Prairie is on the State Park Reservation System from mid-May through mid-September, but no reservations are accepted for Gold Bluffs Beach.

Hiking Activities
More than seventy miles of trails crisscross the park, and sev-

eral of those offer the best hiking in the state parks system for families with toddlers and preschoolers. These are located near the park headquarters and visitor center, and range from less than a half mile in length to about 1.5 miles. All, however, lead you through some of the premier redwood groves in the state. Certainly, they are the most accessible. The shortest of these trails is the 5-Minute Trail, which is a loop trail just behind the visitor center. Near it is the Revelation Trail, a slightly longer loop trail that was developed for the visually impaired and those in wheelchairs; preschoolers enjoy it too. Both are connected by the Redwood Access Trail, which forms a loop with the Nature Trail on the opposite side of Prairie Creek when two seasonal bridges are in place during the summer months.

For older children I prefer to head farther into the park to the north end of Gold Bluffs Beach. There a short one-mile loop trail leads into Fern Canyon where fifty-foot-high rock walls are covered with a lush growth of ferns year-round. If you want a longer hike through the center of the park, you can connect with Irvine Trail at the top of Fern Canyon and continue for another 3.5 miles to the visitors center and the Elk Prairie Campground. This is a good hike, but I recommend it only for those over eight years old.

Another choice hike is the Beach Trail, which continues north from the Fern Canyon Picnic Area for just over two miles to the Butler Creek Backpack Camp and Ossagon Rocks. If you wish to make this an overnight outing, check with the rangers and obtain a permit. The backpack camp is on a first-come, first-served basis, so you should not finalize any plans to overnight there until you get to the park.

If you only want a good day hike, the trek from Fern Canyon to Ossagon Rocks (sea stacks that rise from the pounding surf just offshore and are home to many sea birds) is a great one. The hike is inland from the beach, behind large dunes, and at the base of the high bluffs. Near the rocks you will cross several creeks, and there you may see herds of Roosevelt elk, California's largest land animal.

You may also run across these large animals on the Cathedral Trees Trail, which heads east from the visitor center for just over a mile. This trail leads through groves of the tallest trees in the park, all of which are more than 300 feet high.

Special Outings and Activities

During the summer there is a full range of Junior Ranger programs, ranger-led hikes for both adults and children, and nightly campfire programs. All of these give campers a great introduction to the ecology of the redwood forests, and provide information that you can use as you hike on your own to wild regions of the park.

One don't-miss event at Prairie Creek is the Annual Banana Slug Derby that is held in mid-August. This derby pits the fastest of these slimy creatures against each other in an afternoon of rip-tearing thrills and spills. Well, not exactly, but the children love to catch their own slug to enter in these slow-moving races and they learn about the importance of the banana slug to the ecology of the forest floor.

The Redwood National and State Parks Field Seminars offers many events and classes at Prairie Creek year-round. Check with the Events Coordinator, Redwood National and State Parks Field Seminars, 1111 Second Street, Crescent City, CA 95531; (707) 465-4113, for a catalog of current offerings. Many of these classes fill early, so send for a catalog as soon as you know you are going to be in the region to ensure a spot in the class of your choice. Many of the classes are for kids or for the whole family.

RICHARDSON GROVE STATE PARK
1600 U.S. Highway 101
Garberville, CA 95440
(707) 247-3318

The Eel River runs through this 883-acre redwood park along U.S. 101. Swimming, fishing, rafting, and plenty of hiking trails are all popular activities in the park. There is also a marked nature trail and a visitor center with displays of local

Indian life and local natural history.

Recommended Ages
Excellent for all ages.

Location
The park is eight miles south of Garberville along U.S. 101.

Camping Facilities
Huckleberry, Madrone, and Oak Flat campgrounds contain 169 developed campsites that accommodate twenty-four-foot trailers and thirty-foot motor homes.

Oak Flat lies on the east side of the Eel River and is only open from mid-June to mid-September. This campground differs from the others in the park in that while Huckleberry and Madrone campgrounds are located in tall stands of redwoods, Oak Flat campground sits among a grove of oak where the southern exposure tends to make the campground warm to hot during summer days.

Hiking Activities
Hiking is not the premier activity in this park, but there are several good trails for the whole family. To the north of the Huckleberry campground, the short Woodland Trail loops through a representative section of a redwood forest, and even preschoolers enjoy taking it.

A more rugged Lookout Point Trail leads south from the Madrone campground. Although not much more than a mile-long loop, the trail does climb in elevation to Lookout Point where you can view the Eel River and Oak Flat campground on the opposite side. Preschoolers who are interested hikers can make the climb, however, if you take your time and don't push them too hard.

Two longer trail loops are best for stronger hikers. Kids over nine like to take the Settlers Trail loop out of Oak Flat campground and continue on the Toumey Trail as it leads along the ridge to the east of the Eel River to Panorama Point. This is a great place to stop for a picnic and rest before either continuing on or heading back to the campground. Both directions take about the same amount of time, but you can only complete the loop by crossing the Eel during the summer. Don't attempt to do so when the water is high.

On the west side of the river the Durphy Creek Trail heads west from the Madrone Campground and into the great redwood groves. For a full-day hike, continue on it to Tan Oak Springs Trail for a loop back to Lookout Point Trail. This trek is strictly for older children, or well-conditioned younger children, but it is well worth the effort.

Special Outings and Activities

Since families come to this park in great numbers there are plenty of day and evening activities for everyone. The rangers lead a very active Junior Ranger program, plus many hikes for kids, adults, and whole families. All of these focus on the ecology of the redwood forests of the region and provide plenty of interesting information. Campfire programs are offered nightly during peak season, and the rangers leading the talks actively encourage the kids to participate.

Fishing is a popular activity on the Eel River, and the park roads are good for bicycling.

SALT POINT STATE PARK
25050 Coast Highway 1
Jenner, CA 95450
(707) 847-3221

The four-mile coastline within the park varies from sandy beaches in protected coves to eroded sandstone cliffs. Above the marine terrace where the campgrounds are located is a pygmy forest where pine, cypress, and redwood grow to only a fraction of their normal height. One of the first underwater state parks established in California is in Gerstle Cove.

Recommended Ages
Excellent for all ages.

Location
The park is located along State Route 1 about twenty miles north of Jenner.

Camping Facilities
Moonrock and Woodside campgrounds are the two family campgrounds at Salt Point. In addition, a twenty-site walk-in campground lies about a half-mile from Woodside.

Woodside has eighty developed campsites that accommodate twenty-seven-foot trailers and thirty-one-foot motor homes, and Moonrock has thirty primitive sites that accept twenty-five-foot trailers and motor homes.

There are no showers in either campground, but Woodside does have improved toilets and running water. Moonrock has chemical toilets.

Moonrock is on the ocean side of State Route 1, with easy access to the beaches and cliffs. Woodside lies across the highway from the ocean, but has a trail that leads to the ocean, as well as ones leading uphill to the pygmy forest.

The campgrounds are open all year and on the State Park Reservation System from March through November.

Hiking Activities
Salt Point has some of the most varied hiking of any state park. From trails along the top of the marine terrace in the western portion of the park to Pygmy Forest Trail in the eastern portion, there is hiking for almost all ages and interests.

The trail from Salt Point to Stump Beach Cove leads through the open grasslands of the level marine terrace. It is an easy hike for even preschoolers and toddlers enjoy playing on the sandy beach. The family can make this a 1.5-mile, one-way hike with one parent taking the car to the beach, or a 3-mile loop with the return trek made on the east side of the highway through a redwood forest that is alive with rhododendron blooms in late spring.

My family's favorite hike here is the three-mile loop from Woodside Campground uphill through a stand of redwoods, with trees that rise over 250 feet, to a large open prairie. After walking through the prairie, you enter a surreal world where mature redwood trees, cypress, and pine, which normally range from 150 to 300 feet in height, stand no more than 20 feet high. This stunted growth is the result of the growing conditions present on older marine terraces, where the underlying hardpan prevents proper drainage. The standing water becomes acidic, with a pH similar to that of vinegar, and only certain plants can thrive there. Many that do become so stunted they form the pygmy forests that are found on old terraces up and down the Sonoma and Mendocino coasts.

Shorter trails take hikers around the campgrounds and to Gerstle Cove, where the first underwater state park in California was designated in the 1960s. Scuba divers and snorkelers come to the cove to explore the protected underwater sites, and families like to explore around the rock formations near the cove.

Several trails within the park are designated as equestrian trails, but there are no camping facilities that cater to equestrians.

Special Outings and Activities

The best special activity in this park, a visit to the Pygmy Forest, is discussed above. There is much more for the busy family to do here, though, from climbing on the eroded rocks near the seashore to walking through large thickets of blooming rhododendron to playing on the sandy beach.

The eroded rocks are just north of Gerstle Cove on the western edge of the park, and the sandy beach is Stump Beach, located at the northern terminus of the trail that leads over the marine terrace north of Gerstle Cove. And the rhododendron thickets are found at the northern boundary of the park where it joins the Kruse Rhododendron State Reserve. This reserve has several hundred acres of wild rhododendron that bloom from late April through early June. Kids like to hike along the trails that lead through this tangle of shrubs as they look for small animals and birds.

Redwood parks such as Samuel P. Taylor offer pleasant, shaded camp-grounds and picnic areas.

Small children like to play on the beach, and the barks of harbor seals frequently echo off the bluffs as the seals frolic in the shallow waters of the cove.

SAMUEL P. TAYLOR STATE PARK
P.O. Box 251
Lagunitas, CA 94938
(415) 488-9897

Rolling, grass-covered hills with scattered stands of oak, year-round Papermill (Lagunitas) Creek, and several groves of virgin redwood are all features of this 2,708-acre state park in Marin County. Plenty of trails lead to seldom-used portions of the park, including the top of Mount Barnabe, which was named for a mule of a previous owner of the land.

Swimming, fishing, and hiking are all favorite activities in the park, and exhibits and a marked nature trail offer information about the natural history of the region.

Recommended Ages
Excellent for all ages.

Location
Take Sir Francis Drake Highway fifteen miles west from San Rafael to the park entrance.

Camping Facilities
The campground has sixty-eight sites with showers, water, and toilets, and lies beneath a canopy of old-growth redwoods along Papermill Creek.

Hiking Activities
The campground here sits among tall groves of redwoods along a year-round creek, but the trails lead to a variety of habitats. Those near the campground lead to groves of towering redwoods where a dense understory receives little sunlight because it is filtered by the spreading limbs of the redwoods. As you cross the highway and head up Devil's Gulch and Ridge trails, you enter mixed oak and bay forests along the creeks, and soon reach open grasslands on the slopes of Barnabe Peak.

Tule elk, as well as their larger cousins, Roosevelt elk, roam in large herds in several North Coast parks.

A network of hiking trails and fire roads crisscross the grasslands, and children like to leave the trail to play in the lush green grass during late winter and early spring. By summer the hillsides turn brown and the dry grass is less inviting. The heat of summer keeps most people in the shadows of the redwoods during midday anyway.

The gentle trails that wind through the redwood forest are great for preschoolers and toddlers, who love to explore the fallen logs and small streams found in abundance along them. During warm summer days the flowing waters of Papermill Creek invite youngsters, where they can wade in the shallow areas, and even soak in the deeper pools.

For equestrians there is a corral off Devil's Gulch Trail, and the many fire roads in the park make excellent equestrian trails.

Special Outings and Activities

Watching migrating salmon and steelhead in Papermill Creek, fishing in small pools, and swimming in the deeper pools when the summer days get warm are all popular activities in this park.

Preschoolers love to find rotted or burned redwood stumps and snags and spend endless hours playing in them. These remains often have large cavities the kids can use as houses, where they are joined by pretend playmates of many types.

SINKYONE WILDERNESS STATE PARK
P.O. Box 245
Whitehorn, CA 95489
(707) 986-7711

This wilderness area is located along the Lost Coast of California, a wild and untamed region with few roads and little development. Most people who visit this undeveloped park come for ocean-related activities such as surf fishing, abalone diving, tide pooling, or simply exploring the beaches and cliffs.

The backcountry is accessible only by rugged trails that

only the hardy should attempt, but there is one primitive drive-in campground in the southern portion at Usal Beach.

A large herd of elk roams the hills and meadows of the park and these can best be seen in the spring and fall during rutting and calving times.

Recommended Ages
Poor for toddlers and preschoolers, Good for 6–9, and Excellent for 10 and over.

Location
Extremely isolated, Sinkyone is fifty miles north of Fort Bragg along State Route 1 and County Route 431 or thirty miles west of Redway and U.S. 101 on Briceland Road.

Camping Facilities
Twenty-two secluded, hike-in primitive campsites are located in the northern section of the park, accessible by the Briceland-Whitehorn Road about twenty miles west of Garberville and U.S. 101. There are also trail camps along the fifteen-mile section of Lost Coast Trail that runs along the coast.

At Usal Beach in the southern end of the park there is a fifteen-site primitive campground. You reach this campground by taking State Route 1 north from Rockport for three miles to County Route 431. Turn west on CR 431 and head over six miles of unpaved road to the beach area.

Hiking Activities
Hiking in Sinkyone is a rougher, less-structured activity than in most state parks. The major marked trail is the fifteen-mile Lost Coast Trail, and other treks are along lightly used trails that lead to wilder regions of the park. There you are likely to encounter Roosevelt elk, deer, and other large mammals. If you want to introduce the family to backpacking you can head for any of a number of trail camps located along the Lost Coast Trail for overnights before returning to your base camp at Usal Beach.

The primary recreational activities in the park are ocean related, ranging from surf fishing to tide pooling to walking along the marine terraces where you have great views of the ocean. Favorite hiking areas are along the beaches and atop the marine terraces, which rise above the beaches.

Special Outings and Activities

In general all activities at Sinkyone are special. This is not a developed park where rangers lead programs for families who would rather be entertained by others than find their own activities. Here you must use your own resources, but that isn't necessarily a negative.

The beaches, trails, and open country in this park are not crowded (you may be the only ones in the area), and they offer nature at its best.

Surf fishing is good and wildlife viewing is excellent. With some surf fishing equipment, binoculars, a camera, and a few field guides, I can spend weeks here without needing any guided entertainment.

Throughout the year the Redwood National and State Parks Field Seminars holds occasional events and classes at Sinkyone and other parks in the redwood region. Although only a few courses are offered at Sinkyone, the ones that are offered provide a great opportunity for your family to explore this wild region with a knowledgeable leader. Check with the Events Coordinator, Redwood National and State Parks Field Seminars, 1111 Second Street, Crescent City, CA 95531; (707) 465-4113, for a catalog of current offerings. Many of these classes fill early, so send for a catalog as soon as you know you are going to be in the region to ensure a spot in the class of your choice.

SIX RIVERS NATIONAL FOREST

Forest Supervisor
1330 Bayshore Way
Eureka, CA 95501-3834
(707) 442-1721

This 1,118,247-acre national forest was named from the six major rivers that drain the forest lands—the Smith, Klamath, Trinity, Mad, Van Duzen, and Eel. These rivers provide some of the finest fishing found in the state, and most of the other recreational opportunities in the forest are water oriented.

Backpacking into the rugged back country is another popular attraction of the forest, but the trails are too demanding for most children below their teens. Swimming and float trips are both excellent ways to enjoy the water resources of the forest, and there are ten campgrounds spread throughout the three ranger districts in the lower portion of the forest.

Most of the upper portion of the forest lands is included in the Smith River National Recreation Area, which is a separate entry that immediately follows this one.

Recommended Ages
Poor to Good for toddlers and preschoolers, Good to Excellent for 6–9, and Excellent for 10 and over.

Location
The forest lands stretch south for about 140 miles from the Oregon border in northwestern California. U.S. 101 runs parallel to the western edge of the forest and State Routes 30 and 299 cross the southern and middle portions of it. U.S. 199 crosses the northern portion.

Camping Facilities
Of the ten campgrounds in the Orleans, Lower Trinity, and Mad River ranger districts none are bad. Several, however, are a bit better for families with young children. The best of these are the two campgrounds on the shores of Ruth Lake in remote, western Trinity County. While this site was little known and used until the past several years, families have discovered this beautiful lake.

In recent years the two campgrounds near the lake, Fir Cove and Bailey Canyon, are frequently filled, especially on major holiday weekends, but the forest service has developed an interesting approach to camping there. While you cannot reserve family campsites at any time, the forest service has made Fir Cove into a group camp Monday through Thursday of each week. During this time the campground is divided into three large group sites of six or seven individual campsites. The large sites can be reserved in advance, and there is a set rate of $25 to $35 per night for them. Any size group may reserve a site, including a large family that likes to spread out. On Friday, Saturday, and Sunday the campground reverts to a normal family campground with no reservations.

Between the two campgrounds, you should be able to find a site midweek during the summer, but if you can't, you can find one at the Mad River Campground about two miles north of Ruth Lake along the Mad River, from mid-May through mid-October.

My personal favorite in the national forest is a small, twenty-three-unit campground that lies deep within Bigfoot country along the shores of Fish Lake. This small jewel of a lake provides good trout fishing for stocked rainbow, and the campground is heavily used from Memorial Day through early July, but few people venture into this area the rest of the year.

When the crowds are small, this is a great place for families with children from toddlers to teens. The shallow lake offers excellent fishing opportunities for blue gill and other pan fish, children like to explore around its edges for aquatic animals, and teens can canoe or raft on the gentle waters during midday.

For families who want to backpack as part of their vacation, the Six Rivers National Forest includes one of the premier backpacking areas in the West. The Trinity Alps Wilderness Area includes ragged granite peaks, alpine lakes, and cold mountain streams, all with few crowds.

There are also two other wilderness areas in the forest, Siskiyou and Yolla Bolly–Middle Eel, but I am less familiar with them. I do know that the Yolla Bolly gets quite hot during midsummer, and backpacking in the region then becomes difficult.

Hiking Activities

There are hundreds of miles of hiking trails maintained by the forest service that lead through dense redwood and Douglas fir forests in the national forest. Some of these lead from the campground areas, take you along streams and rivers, then to the tops of ridges where you'll encounter openings in the forest that provide you with panoramic vistas.

You can find out about other trails away from the campgrounds by asking the rangers. Many of these take you into some of the wildest country in the state. Even if you don't run across Bigfoot, if you hike for any distance you're likely to encounter at least one black bear.

Special Outings and Activities

Spawning salmon, black bear, one of the largest concentrations of deer in California, and dense groves of gigantic redwoods all make the whole national forest a special outing for me. For your own special outing you will have to explore the region and find what most intrigues you and your family.

If fishing is something your family enjoys, you will find it year-round in the streams, rivers, and lakes of the region. If hiking is your thing, there is no lack of it anywhere you head. From an easy stroll to a difficult trek, you can find a hike that any age child will enjoy.

If you would rather boat or swim than fish or hike, you will find abundant opportunities in this region.

SMITH RIVER NATIONAL RECREATION AREA
10600 Highway 199
Gasquet, CA 95543-0228
(707) 457-3131

Due east of Crescent City a large portion of the Six Rivers National Forest is so filled with recreational opportunities that the national forest has declared it a national recreation area.

Hiking, camping, fishing, backpacking, and rafting—name an outdoor activity and chances are you can find it in the Smith River National Recreation Area.

Recommended Ages
Poor to Good for toddlers and preschoolers, Good to Excellent for 6–9, and Excellent for 10 and over.

Location
The area extends from the Oregon border south to the Klamath River, and includes a huge section of the Siskiyou Mountains. U.S. 199 crosses the northern half of the recreation area, as does State Route 299, and several minor roads take visitors into the interior of it. For the adventurous, a number of maintained, dirt forest service roads lead even farther from civilization.

Camping Facilities
There are four developed campgrounds in the recreation area, but one, Grassy Flat, sits along U.S. 199 across the highway from a CalTrans waste area. It is noisy, crowded, and not really conducive for a great family outing.

Patrick Creek Campground is situated in a much more beautiful setting, also along U.S. 199, at the confluence of Patrick Creek and the Smith River. This small, seventeen-site campground sits next to the rustic Patrick Creek Lodge and is only a short drive from the Siskiyou Wilderness.

Panther Flat Campground, with forty-two sites, has more room and is not as close to civilization as is Patrick Creek. It is also located near U.S. 199 and offers ready access to Jedediah Smith State Park, Redwood National Park, and the Siskiyou Wilderness.

My favorite campground in the recreation area is more isolated, however, and its forty sites are seldom filled. Big Flat Campground sits beside Hurdy-Gurdy Creek about fifteen miles from U.S. 199, and there is something here for the whole family. The Hurdy-Gurdy flows into the Smith River near the campground, and fishing, swimming, kayaking, and rafting are all popular activities here. There is also access to the Old Kelsey Trail, a great backpacking and hiking route, from the campground.

Hiking Activities
The primary hiking here is done on the Old Kelsey Trail out of Big Flat Campground, but there is hiking near all of the campgrounds. The Siskiyou Wilderness, which is accessible from all the campgrounds in the recreation area, also offers great hiking for those who want more strenuous trails.

Special Outings and Activities
Visits to state and national redwood forests, campfires at the larger campgrounds, watching for spawning salmon in season, and just enjoying the solitude of the redwood forests are what make this region special.

SONOMA COAST STATE BEACH
Bodega Bay, CA 94923
(707) 875-3483

This is actually a series of beaches separated by steep bluffs that extend thirteen miles from Bodega Head to the south to the Russian River to the north. Dune walks, strolls across the flat grasslands atop marine terraces, and lazing on the beaches are all popular activities here.

Two drive-in and two walk-in campgrounds are part of the park, and they offer great opportunities to explore the ocean shore and inland redwood groves.

Recommended Ages
Excellent for all ages.

Location
Along State Route 1 from Bodega Bay north to the Russian River.

Camping doesn't have to be far from populated areas to get away from crowds, as this shot from near San Francisco shows.

Camping Facilities

Two drive-in campgrounds, Bodega Dunes and Wrights Beach, offer more than 125 sites near the ocean. Bodega Dunes has 98 developed sites with showers, and accommodates thirty-one-foot trailers and motor homes. Wrights Beach has 30 developed campsites, but no showers, and accommodates twenty-seven-foot trailers and motor homes.

In addition to the two drive-in campgrounds there are two environmental campgrounds, Willow Creek and Pomo Canyon, in this park unit. These campgrounds are several hundred yards from a parking area. You must bring your own water to Willow Creek, and at Pomo Canyon water is available about fifty yards from the campsites. Both of these campgrounds are several miles from the ocean, but, consequently, are less likely to be filled.

The campgrounds are open all year and on the State Park Reservation System year-round.

Hiking Activities

In this park unit you have choice of hiking among sand dunes, atop marine terraces, or through grasslands to redwood forests. Which is closest depends on the campground you choose. At Bodega Dunes Campground your choices are more than five miles of trails among the dunes and along three-mile-long Salmon Creek Beach. For a little longer hike you can leave the dunes and hike across scrub-covered hills past the Bodega Marine Lab to Bodega Head. There you can watch for migrating whales or hike around the head watching for harbor seals that hang out on offshore rocks.

From Wrights Beach Campground you can head either north or south along the marine terraces on the Kortum Trail. This trail follows the length of the thirteen miles of the park unit from Goat Rock in the north to Bodega Head in the south. Since Wright's Beach is about halfway between the two, you can hike as far as you like, stopping at little-used, sheltered beaches along the way. The terraces are carpeted with wildflowers in the spring, and birders like to keep an eye out for various raptors, including red-tailed hawk and osprey, who fly over the flat grasslands in search of prey.

Just north of Wright's Beach on State Route 1 is Shell Beach, and from the parking lot there you can take a 2.5-mile hike over the ridge to Pomo Canyon Environmental Campground. This hike takes you over the first ridge and through open grassland, where you have great views of the ocean and the mouth of the Russian River at Goat Rock Beach to the north. As you reach the flat terrace you begin to overlook the Russian River Valley to the north, and soon enter a redwood forest before you drop down into Pomo Canyon. This is also an excellent hike to the beach if you are camped at Pomo Canyon.

The best campground and hiking area if you have preschoolers or toddlers is Bodega Dunes, because they can play in protected sand dunes or along the wide Salmon Creek Beach.

Special Outings and Activities
Special activities here include whale watching from the bluffs at Bodega Head and along the marine terraces farther north,

visiting with harbor seals at their haul-out (an area where seals leave the water and lay on shore) at the mouth of the Russian River at Goat Rock Beach (they give birth to their young in March and April), exploring the peaks and valleys of the dunes, and looking for the butterfly bush where thousands of Monarch butterflies gather in December to spend the winter.

Ranger-led walks are held during peak season, and campfires most nights in midsummer. These give campers ideas about where to go and what to do in this long, narrow park along State Route 1.

STANDISH-HICKEY STATE RECREATION AREA
P.O. Box 208
Leggett, CA 95455
(707) 925-6482

Steep trails that wind through a river canyon, dense groves of second-growth redwoods, and swimming holes fifteen to twenty feet deep in the South Fork of the Eel River attract visitors to this 1,020-acre park.

Although close to the highway, this is one of the least visited state redwood parks. This does not mean that there isn't plenty for the whole family to enjoy, though, as the park has almost two miles of river frontage and a 225-foot redwood, called the Miles Standish tree, with a 40-foot circumference. It's estimated to be 1,200 years old.

Recommended Ages
Good for toddlers and preschoolers, and Excellent for 6–9 and for 10 and over.

Location
The park is off U.S. 101 about a mile north of Leggett.

Camping Facilities
Three campgrounds, with a total of 162 campsites, are spread throughout this park. Hickey and Rock Creek Camp-

grounds accommodate twenty-four-foot trailers and twenty-seven-foot motor homes in developed sites with showers nearby. Redwood Campground is more isolated and the narrow, steep road limits trailers and motor homes to eighteen feet.

Hickey and Rock Creek are open year-round, but Redwood Campground is open only in the summer because the bridge leading to it is removed during the winter.

Hickey and Rock Creek are on the State Park Reservation System from May through September, and Redwood from mid-June through mid-September.

Hiking Activities

Almost ten miles of trails lead through the redwood groves in this park. One of the best short hikes doesn't lead from the campground but is located across U.S. 101 from the park entrance. The trailhead to Ray and Talsma meadows is well marked beside the highway, and the trail leads uphill through the two meadows before it loops around a grove of large redwoods. Hardy preschoolers enjoy this hike, as do older children.

Older children like to hike along the Big Tree Trail through Cabin Meadow above the South Fork of the Eel River to the Captain Miles Standish Tree, the giant mentioned above.

This hike is an excellent half-day outing for most, making a loop by returning on the upper portion of the trail, but those who want to make a full-day hike can continue on the Mill Creek Trail as it follows above the river and loops around a spectacular landslide area before rejoining the Big Tree Trail. You can then return by the lower or upper portion of the trail as you like.

Short trails lead from the campgrounds on the bluffs above the river down to the water where everyone from toddlers to parents can explore along the slow-moving river in the summer. During the winter and spring the waters roar down the canyon and are popular with fishermen and kayakers.

Special Outings and Activities

During midsummer the weather can get quite warm in this park, consequently a favorite activity here is swimming in the South Fork of the Eel River as it meanders north. High bluffs rise above the fifteen- to twenty-foot holes carved into the river's bed, and large boulders offer great diving spots. Make sure the water is reconnoitered for underwater hazards before you let anyone dive, but other than that there is nothing to keep the whole family from enjoying an afternoon or two or three when it's just too hot to do anything else. Preschoolers and toddlers enjoy the shallower pools, where they can splash and search for small aquatic creatures.

In early morning and late evening many people fish along the banks of the river, and some children like to dip their hooks even in midday when there is little chance of catching anything.

Preschoolers like to find a cool grove of redwoods where fires have carved out large cavities in the huge tree trunks. They while away hours in their pretend castles and forts.

During peak season there are frequent campfires where rangers talk about the history and ecology of the region. There are also ranger-led hikes occasionally.

SUGARLOAF RIDGE STATE PARK
2605 Adobe Canyon Road
Kenwood, CA 95452
(707) 833-5712

Peaks that reach almost 3,000 feet toward the sky, steep canyons with seasonal streams, open grasslands where wildflowers proliferate during late spring, and plenty of deer and rattlesnake are all found in this park. The elevations in the 2,373-acre park vary from 600 feet at the entrance to 2,729 at the top of Bald Mountain, where you have great views of the Sierra Nevada and San Francisco Bay on clear days.

The park is a popular horseback riding site, and a local concessionaire leads trail rides for those who don't have their own horses.

Recommended Ages
Good for toddlers and preschoolers, and Excellent for 6–9 and for 10 and over.

Location
Head seven miles east of Santa Rosa on State Route 12 and then three miles north on Adobe Canyon Road to the park.

Camping Facilities
This campground has fifty developed sites, but no showers. Fifteen sites accommodate twenty-four-foot trailers and twenty-seven-foot motor homes. Equestrian camping facilities, with corrals and water troughs, are also available.

The campground is open year-round and on the State Park Reservation System all year.

Hiking Activities
Trails in this park follow creeks down fern canyons, cross meadows carpeted with spring wildflowers, and climb to the top of rounded peaks from which you can see the San Francisco Bay and the Sierra Nevada on clear days.

The Creekside Nature Trail leads out from the campground and is a delightful hike for toddlers and preschoolers. Even older kids like to take this self-guided trail to learn about the ecology of the park.

A slightly longer and more arduous trail loop from the campgrounds is the Pony Gate/Canyon Trail loop. I take the Pony Gate Trail as it heads downhill and then loops across the park road before ascending up the Sonoma Creek Canyon. After the winter rains this canyon is filled with lush ferns and moss covered rocks, and the creek cascades over large boulders to spray hikers who venture too near. As the creek level drops the trail provides a cool hike during warm (even hot) summer days.

Before the summer heat, which often exceeds 100 degrees in the park, descends on the slopes of the peaks, the trails that transect the meadows offer great hikes. Older kids like to climb through the oak and digger pine forests to the chaparral-covered slopes where they have panoramic views.

If you come to the park in the early spring you will find meadows carpeted with wildflowers, but danger also lurks when the first warm days come to the region. Nowhere else in Northern California are you as likely to encounter rattlesnakes as you are in this park. In fact, this is where I head with groups when I want to introduce children to this much-maligned animal.

Although the sight and sound of this venomous snake brings terror to most people, I find it an intriguing animal. They pose little danger if you follow proper outdoor etiquette and don't place the snakes in a position where they feel they must strike out.

If you keep toddlers and preschoolers in the campground and around the creek you have little to fear from rattlers in the park. It is only when you venture into the rocky areas above the campground that you are likely to encounter the creatures.

Special Outings and Activities
Playing in the creek, searching for aquatic creatures, and hiking are all favorite activities here. Keep an eye out for rattlesnakes as you hike around the park. While I feel that these generally reclusive creatures are likely to cause more excitement than harm, exercise caution in their habitat. Rangers give campfire talks about them and provide information about where they are most likely to be seen, more as an advisory about the dangers associated with the snake than as an encouragement to go searching for them.

Rangers lead hikes for kids and whole families at times, and campfires are presented frequently during peak season.

VAN DAMME STATE PARK
P.O. Box 440
Mendocino, CA 95460
(707) 937-5804

At Van Damme State Park you can explore along the beach, hike through Fern Canyon, and learn why cone-bearing pine and cypress stand only six inches to eight feet tall in the Pygmy Forest above the park. Visitors also come here to hike, fish, and just enjoy nature.

Recommended Ages
Good for toddlers and preschoolers, and Excellent for 6–9 and for 10 and over.

Location
The entrance to the park is three miles south of the village of Mendocino along State Route 1.

Camping Facilities
Highland Meadow and Lower campgrounds offer seventy-four developed sites and showers in this park. Highland Meadow is located high above the Little River Canyon, while Lower Campground lies beside the river. There are also ten hike-in campsites about 1.75 miles up the river from the parking area.

The campgrounds accommodate eighteen-foot trailers and twenty-one-foot motor homes. The sites are open year-round and on the State Park Reservation System from April through mid-October.

Hiking Activities
Two major hiking trails and a short boardwalk trail are the primary features of this park. From the campground center Fern Canyon heads upstream through lush vegetation along the Little River. This trail continues uphill to the Pygmy Forest where everyone can view the stunted trees that grow to less than a tenth of what they normally do. From the Pygmy Forest, Old Logging Road Trail leads back downhill to rejoin Fern Canyon Trail.

If you're with younger children and don't want to make the long hike uphill, you can drive to the beginning of the

Pygmy Forest self-guided trail. From the parking area take the short walk through the forest, and those who want to take the hike downhill can do so as the others return to the campground area by car.

The trail along Little River also leads from the campground area to the small beach at the mouth of the river. Toddlers and preschoolers like to play along the rocky shore, but the water is generally too cold to swim in.

Special Outings and Activities

Playing on the small beach, wading along the shallow pools of the Little River, and exploring for frogs and dragonflies around the edges of the Cabbage Patch, a bog where skunk cabbage grows in abundance, are all popular activities here.

There is a visitor center and museum, and rangers lead hikes during the day for both kids and whole families. Kids can also participate in the Junior Ranger program during the day. Campfire programs at night provide information about the history and ecology of the area.

In late July the park sponsors a weekend of Logging History Days, when visitors can learn about the lives and lore of the rugged loggers who cut and milled some of the largest trees in the world during the latter half of the nineteenth century. Displays of early logging equipment and tools are featured, and living history demonstrations often include visitors as participants. Both children and adults enjoy this lively celebration.

CHAPTER 2

NORTH INLAND CAMPING

When you cross over the rugged ridges of the northern Coast Range you leave the towering redwood forests and enter thick conifer forests where the shapely Douglas firs tower high above stands of oak, bay, and chaparral. These slowly thin out as you continue eastward.

In the northern end of the Sacramento Valley several large reservoirs provide recreational opportunities ranging from fishing to waterskiing, but many campers prefer to head for the higher elevations of the southern Cascades and northern Sierra. There campgrounds sit beside cold mountain streams and blue lakes.

No other region of California is so diverse in its outdoor offerings. In the north are dormant volcanoes and vast lava fields, wetlands that provide home to some of the largest congregations of waterfowl in the nation, the largest flocks of bald eagles in the lower forty-eight states, and the best trout fishing in the world.

Farther south the Cascades give way to the Sierra Nevada with high alpine lakes, outstanding trails, vibrant wildflower displays, and the glacier-carved granite cliffs of Yosemite and the High Sierra.

During the winter, campers head for campgrounds in the

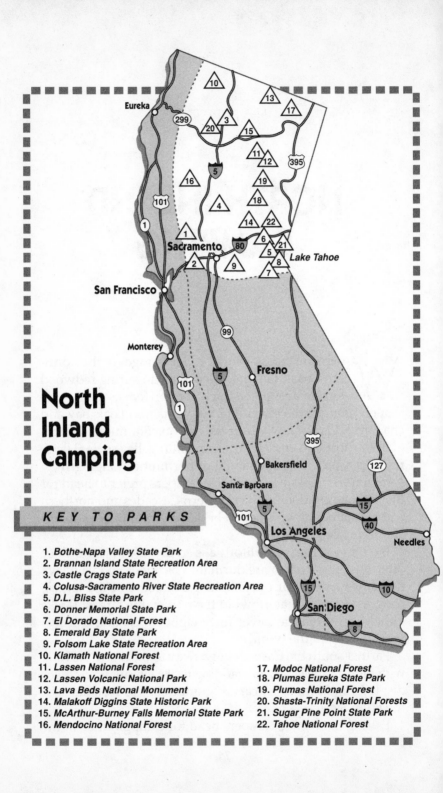

North Inland Camping

KEY TO PARKS

1. *Bothe-Napa Valley State Park*
2. *Brannan Island State Recreation Area*
3. *Castle Crags State Park*
4. *Colusa-Sacramento River State Recreation Area*
5. *D.L. Bliss State Park*
6. *Donner Memorial State Park*
7. *El Dorado National Forest*
8. *Emerald Bay State Park*
9. *Folsom Lake State Recreation Area*
10. *Klamath National Forest*
11. *Lassen National Forest*
12. *Lassen Volcanic National Park*
13. *Lava Beds National Monument*
14. *Malakoff Diggins State Historic Park*
15. *McArthur-Burney Falls Memorial State Park*
16. *Mendocino National Forest*
17. *Modoc National Forest*
18. *Plumas Eureka State Park*
19. *Plumas National Forest*
20. *Shasta-Trinity National Forests*
21. *Sugar Pine Point State Park*
22. *Tahoe National Forest*

Central Valley where they can see gatherings of tundra swan and sandhill crane, as well as up to a million Canada geese.

All in all, the North Inland section of California is a camper's paradise that offers great outings for families.

BOTHE-NAPA VALLEY STATE PARK
3801 St. Helena Highway North
Calistoga, CA 94515
(707) 942-4575

This 1,917-acre state park has redwood forests, fern canyons, live streams, seasonal waterfalls, and great hiking and horse-back riding trails. Families will enjoy swimming in Ritchey Creek during the summer after a day hike. This small creek flows through a redwood forest. The shade of the giant trees offers a break from the high temperatures that are frequent in mid-summer here.

Recommended Ages
Excellent for all ages.

Location
The park is four miles north of St. Helena on State Route 29/128.

Camping Facilities
The Ritchey Creek Campground has fifty developed camp-sites (ten of these are walk-in sites) and a hike and bike campground. These sheltered sites are situated along Ritchey Creek in some of the most easterly stands of redwoods in California. Surrounding the campground area the redwoods are intermixed with stands of Douglas fir, tan oak, and ma-drone.

Showers are scattered throughout the campground, and the sites accommodate twenty-four-foot trailers and thirty-one-foot motor homes. The campground is open and on the State Park Reservation System all year.

Hiking Activities

While none of the trails in this park offer miles and miles of uninterrupted hiking, several do take you into dense redwood groves. There you'll find Ritchey Creek rushing down over rock outcroppings to form misty falls that children like to play around, particularly in the summer when the temperatures are high. Other trails lead to chaparral-covered hills from which you have great views of the wine country in the northern end of the Napa Valley.

The trails along Ritchey Creek are good outings for toddlers and preschoolers because they can play in the creek when it is low or toss leaves and twigs into the rushing water during the winter.

Special Outings and Activities

This is one of the few state parks with a maintained and supervised swimming pool, and children of all ages enjoy it during the hot summer months. There is also a small dam across Ritchey Creek, which forms a wading pool where youngsters can play.

Although the fishing in the creek is not what an adult would call acceptable, young children like to fish in some of the deeper holes. They come up with crawdads and small fish often enough to make the fishing interesting.

A history trail leads from the visitor center, where there are exhibits of local ecology and history, past a picnic area, around a pioneer cemetery, and to the Bale Grist Mill State Historic Park. There the whole family can enjoy exploring a restored mill that offers a glimpse of early California life. In mid-October more than one thousand people congregate at the mill to celebrate Old Mill Days. There they enjoy reenactments of how people lived in the Napa Valley in the mid-1800s.

During the summer, rangers frequently offer campfire talks where they tell stories of both the natural and the human history of the region.

BRANNAN ISLAND STATE RECREATION AREA
17645 Highway 160
Rio Vista, CA 94571
(916) 777-6671

The Sacramento/San Joaquin Delta has over a thousand miles of rivers, sloughs, levees, marshes, and old river channels in a thousand-mile rectangle between Sacramento and San Francisco.

The only public campground within this large area is Brannan Island State Recreation Area on Three Mile Slough off the Sacramento River. Visitors to the region enjoy fishing, swimming, boating, and bicycle riding.

Recommended Ages
Good for all ages.

Location
The recreation area is on State Route 160 along the east side of the Sacramento River, thirteen miles northeast of Antioch and four miles south of Rio Vista.

Camping Facilities
This recreation area's campgrounds have 102 developed sites along Three Mile Slough just before it joins the Sacramento River. The campgrounds are open and have little shelter from the hot summer sun of the Sacramento Valley.

The sites accommodate thirty-one-foot trailers and motor homes and are fully developed except for showers. There is little difference between Cottonwood and Willow campgrounds, which are separated by a campfire circle where ranger talks are frequently presented.

The campgrounds are open year-round and on the State Park Reservation System from February through October.

Hiking Activities
There are no formal hiking trails in the recreation area, but children like to hike along the levees that restrain the waters

of Three Mile and Seven Mile sloughs. At several locations they can head down to the water's edge, where small aquatic animals are found in abundance.

A walk along lightly traveled Twitchell Island Road takes you away from the recreation area and into the farming regions of the delta. This is a pleasant walk and in addition to viewing the large farms you may also see a wide variety of bird life, for which the delta region is justly famous.

Special Outings and Activities

Water activities predominate the action here. From swimming in the shallows of Seven Mile Slough to fishing along the sloughs and the Sacramento River, there is a water activity for every member of the family.

Many families who camp here bring their boats. After launching them at the boat ramp they can then explore the many miles of waterways nearby, fish along the slough and river, or water ski in the more open areas.

Fishing is also good to excellent from the banks of the sloughs, and many people while away whole days keeping their lines baited and in the water.

During the summer months park rangers give frequent campfire talks where they discuss the delta's human and natural history.

CASTLE CRAGS STATE PARK
P.O. Box 80
Castella, CA 96017
(916) 235-2684 or 225-2065

Ancient granite spires, two miles of the upper Sacramento River, and seven miles of the Pacific Crest Trail are features of this northern California park. Hiking is by far the most popular activity here, but geology enthusiasts like to explore the granite spires, which also attract some climbers. Trout fishing is good to excellent in the river, but the water is a bit too cold for swimming for long periods.

Several backcountry hikes offer great views of Mt. Shasta

to the north. Elevations range from about two thousand feet along the river to over six thousand feet at the top of the crags.

Recommended Ages
Poor for toddlers and preschoolers, and Excellent for 6–9 and for 10 and over.

Location
The park is off I-5 about six miles south of Dunsmuir.

Camping Facilities
From the campground at this park you have great views of 14,162-foot Mt. Shasta to the north, and the cool waters of the upper reaches of the Sacramento River are just a short walk away.

There are sixty-four developed sites in the campground, and three small environmental campsites nearby for those who wish to walk in a ways. All are sheltered from the sun at least part of the day, and are midway between Root and Indian creeks.

Showers are scattered throughout the campground, and the sites accommodate twenty-one-foot trailers and twenty-seven-foot motor homes.

The campground is open and on the State Park Reservation System year-round.

Hiking Activities
Hiking is the predominate family activity at this park. From the short loop of the Indian Creek Trail to the longer Crags Trail, there is a hike for everyone here. Of interest to older children is the Pacific Crest Trail that bisects the park. Hiking along this well-known trail, which extends from the Canadian to the Mexican border, becomes a special event, and many older children like to take an overnight hike along the trail away from the campground.

I like to cross under I-5 via the pedestrian undercrossing and hike along the River Trail that leads along this stretch of the upper Sacramento River. This hike is particularly beautiful in the spring when the wildflowers are out and in the fall when the leaves on deciduous trees have turned brilliant colors.

Special Outings and Activities
I mentioned the special outing with a hike along the Pacific Crest Trail, but fishing in Castle Creek and the Sacramento River are also extremely popular. Younger children like to fish in Root and Indian creeks, which also provide shallow pools for younger children to play in and cool off on hot summer afternoons.

For adults, a favorite activity is to place a camp chair in just the right position to view the snow covered peak of Mt. Shasta just to the north. I can spend long hours just quietly viewing this quiescent volcano, imagining the powerful forces that formed the surrounding region.

COLUSA-SACRAMENTO RIVER STATE RECREATION AREA
P.O. Box 207
Colusa, CA 95932
(916) 458-4927

This small recreation area is primarily used by fishermen and hunters, but families can enjoy a stay here. There is good access to a stretch of the Sacramento River, a trail through an undisturbed riparian forest, and easy access to several national wildlife refuges where you can see migrating waterfowl during the fall and winter months.

Recommended Ages
Good for toddlers and preschoolers, Excellent for 6–9, and Good for 10 and over.

Location
This site is located near downtown Colusa along the Sacramento River. Colusa is nine miles east of I-5 on State Route 20.

Walks along rivers and waterways, such as this one along the Sacramento River at Colusa State Recreation Area, are pleasant ways to spend lazy afternoons.

Camping Facilities

The small campground here sits beside a large curve in the Sacramento River. Only ten of the twenty-two sites are fully developed with tables and fire pits, but all are roomy enough for large families or twenty-four-foot trailers and twenty-seven-foot motor homes.

The campground is open and on the State Park Reservation System year-round.

Hiking Activities

Hiking is limited in this recreation area, but there is one excellent hike through an undisturbed riparian forest with cottonwood that reach more than 100 feet into the air. The hike leads through the dense understory where birds and other wildlife thrive. This is one of the few places left in California where you can hear the call of the yellow-billed cuckoo.

The hike returns to the campground along the banks of the Sacramento River, where the children can toss rocks into the fast-flowing water and watch for birds such as the great blue heron that come to the river to feed. Tadpoles thrive in the quieter pools near the shore, and other aquatic animals can also be found there.

For a different type of walk, head down the levee as it continues along the river past the town of Colusa. You can see how the town sits below the water level of the river and imagine how devastating it was when the river flowed over the levee in 1955–1956. The flood level has not reached that height since, but it is likely it will again in the future.

Special Outings and Activities

The special outings here revolve around the national wildlife refuges within easy driving distance of the campground. During the fall and winter huge flocks of waterfowl use the fields and ponds of these refuges to rest and feed during their migration south. Some even stop here for the winter.

From November through March you can see as many as a million waterfowl at a time in the Sacramento National Wildlife Refuge just to the northwest of Colusa. Several other state and federal refuges are also nearby. Although it can be cold during that period, children like to come to the region to see the waterfowl and then camp for a night or two along the river.

Fishing is good in the river during the summer, and many fishermen use the campground. If you come during midweek, though, you can get a site and enjoy bank fishing if you don't have a small boat to launch at the park.

D.L. BLISS STATE PARK
P.O. Box 266
Tahoma, CA 95733
(916) 525-7277

One of several large state parks in the Tahoe Basin, this popular 1,237-acre park has a marked nature trail, several miles of high country trails, a lighthouse, and good swimming. Over six miles of Lake Tahoe shoreline are within the boundaries of this park and the adjoining Emerald Bay State Park.

Recommended Ages
Excellent for all ages.

Location
The park is off State Route 89, seventeen miles south of Tahoe City.

Camping Facilities
This is one of the most scenic campgrounds in California, since it sits just north of Emerald Bay on the shore of Lake Tahoe. The 168 developed campsites are generally full, but you can make reservations through the State Park Reservation System.

The campground is divided into four units, and if you want to be close to the beach try to get into sites 141–168 when you make your reservations. The next choice would be sites 1–90, where you also have easy access to the Rubicon Trail to Emerald Point.

The campground is open and on the State Park Reservation System from mid-June to Labor Day.

Hiking Activities
The Balancing Rock self-guided nature trail is great for preschoolers and even toddlers. The Old Lighthouse trail is popular for strong preschoolers and older children, leading from the campground to Calawee Cove Beach.

For longer hikes, take the Rubicon Trail as it leads from Calawee Cove south for 4.5 miles past Emerald Point to the Vikingsholm at Emerald Bay.

Special Outings and Activities
Rangers offer campfire talks almost every night during the summer and lead hikes for both children and adults during the day. Children can also join in on Junior Ranger activities during the day to give parents a break.

Although the waters of Lake Tahoe are very cold (they really are recently melted snow that runs into a 1,600-foot-deep lake where only the most shallow waters ever warm) children do like to swim in the shallows along the beach at Calawee Cove. Just north of the cove lies Lester Beach, another favorite swimming spot.

Fishing in Lake Tahoe is best from offshore boats, but the kids like to fish in the deeper holes along the shoreline away from the beaches. There they may catch a trout or two, plus some pan fish in the warmer waters.

DONNER MEMORIAL STATE PARK
P.O. Box 9210
Truckee, CA 95737
(916) 587-3841

Geologic and human history abound within this 353-acre park on the shores of Donner Lake. A museum recounts the tragic tale of the Donner Party, and the large slabs of exposed granite tell of early geological activities in the region.

Hiking, swimming, and lazing in the sun are favorite activities of campers here.

Recommended Ages
Excellent for all ages.

Location
On Donner Pass Road, two miles west of Truckee.

Camping Facilities
This park has three campgrounds with 154 developed campsites. Showers are scattered throughout the campgrounds, which accommodate twenty-four-foot trailers and twenty-eight-foot motor homes. Splitrock Campground has easiest access to the swimming area, which makes it good for families with older children, but the other two are not that far from the water.

The park is open and on the State Park Reservation System from mid-May to mid-September.

Hiking Activities

For younger children the hike along the nature trail along Donner Creek behind the museum is perfect, while older ones enjoy the hike along the China Cove trail from Splitrock Campground to the swimming area. Other marked trails lead from the campground into areas of exposed granite where you can see the results of the violent geological history of the Sierra.

Special Outings and Activities

Swimming in the cool, but tolerable, waters of Donner Lake is excellent along the two-plus miles of beach near the campgrounds, and fishing is good in the coves and shallow pools away from the beaches.

Just about all children are fascinated by the exhibits at the museum in the park that documents the doomed winter of the Donner Party. Rangers can help you locate sites uphill from the park where the Donner Party camped in their ill-fated effort to cross the pass during a heavy winter.

EL DORADO NATIONAL FOREST

Forest Supervisor
100 Forni Road
Placerville, CA 95667
(916) 622-5061

The two popular wilderness areas and four ranger districts in this forest offer outstanding outdoor recreational opportunities. Swimming, hiking, and fishing are all popular in the forest, and forty campgrounds are spread throughout the area.

This is one of the most productive national forests in the West for timber, and logging activities are seen through the spring, summer, and fall.

Recommended Ages

Good to Excellent for all ages.

Parents frequently have to carry an extra load on camping hikes.

Location

The forest lies to the east of Sacramento and southeast of Lake Tahoe. U.S. 50 runs through the middle of the forest and many of the campgrounds are accessible from it. Other campsites are closer to State Route 88 further south.

Camping Facilities

With forty campgrounds to choose from in this large national forest, it's hard to make recommendations about which ones to pick. I wish my family lived nearby so we could try all of them out one at a time, but we don't so I just have to return to the ones I most appreciate.

In the Georgetown Ranger District I recommend Big Meadows Campground, with fifty-five developed sites that accept trailers and motor homes, near Hell Hole Reservoir, and Stumpy Meadows Campground, with forty developed sites that accept trailers and motor homes, near Stumpy Meadows Reservoir. Both of these are full service campgrounds, and children like to fish and swim in the nearby reservoirs.

A less developed and more isolated campground is located

along the eastern end of Hell Hole Reservoir. When I want to get away from the crowds I take my family to the fifteen-site Upper Hell Hole Campground where there are pit toilets and no accommodations for trailers or motor homes, and where the only water is from a nearby stream.

In the Pacific Ranger District I particularly like the Loon Lake Campground. This thirty-four-site campground sits beside a beautiful Sierra lake at 6,500 feet, where you can escape from the torrid summer heat of the Sacramento Valley. Other good campgrounds are located near Union Valley and Ice House reservoirs.

In the Placerville Ranger District the twenty-three-site China Flat and thirty-five-site Silver Fork campgrounds are next to the South Fork of the American River, between U.S. 50 and State Route 88. Both campgrounds offer great camping along a beautiful mountain river.

In the Amador Ranger District the South Shore Campground on the shores of the Lower Bear River Reservoir is a great place to camp in early spring and late fall when the campgrounds at the higher elevations are closed. But when summer comes I head for Upper and Lower Blue lakes, which lie at over 8,000 feet elevation. All of these campgrounds have approximately twenty-five developed sites and are located in outstanding scenic areas.

For years, my favorite campground in this district was the one at Woods Lake near Carson Pass. This campground sits alongside a beautiful alpine lake and trout fishing is good on the creek that empties from the lake near the campground. The last time I visited the campground, though, I felt that it had become too large for its setting. It remains a great place to camp and hike to even higher alpine lakes such as Winnemucca, 4th of July, and Round Top.

Most of the campgrounds I mentioned above are only open from about June to October, some for even shorter periods, because of the heavy winters of the Sierra. Always check with the ranger district where you are heading to see if the campgrounds are open.

Hiking Activities

Hiking in the national forest is almost unlimited. From trails that lead around lakes and reservoirs to ones that lead far into wilderness areas, where the land is as wild as it was during the days before Europeans invaded the state, there is a trail for just about everyone.

Many of the trails into wilderness areas lead to scenic locations, and the trail from the forest service information center at Carson Pass is one of the best. It leads past Frog Lake and across a high mountain meadow where wildflowers are so profuse in the spring and summer that the USFS has designated the area a protected area and natural site.

This is also a great trail to introduce youngsters to the pleasures of backpacking. Frog Lake is less than a mile in, and Winnemucca and Round Top are other stops within a three-mile stretch where you can camp overnight.

Special Outings and Activities

Special outings in the national forest tend to be associated with water. Reservoirs, high alpine lakes, and ice-cold rivers and streams attract fisherman throughout the summer. The larger reservoirs attract boaters and water-skiers.

Even if you don't participate in water sports there is something magical about camping alongside a cold mountain lake where motor boats are not allowed. You wake in the morning with the sun reflecting off the lake's surface, and in the afternoon cool winds blow in off the lake as the sun begins to set behind the high ridges to the west. Any boats on the lake glide silently over the still waters, leaving ever-widening ripples in their wake. These quiet, slow-moving craft seem to be a part of the natural surroundings, unlike their noisy motorized counterparts. In between, you can explore the water's edge, hike along the streams in search of aquatic animals, and if you are really lucky you may come upon a meadow where beaver have dammed the stream. There you can try to catch a glimpse of these reclusive creatures at dusk when they come out to feed.

EMERALD BAY STATE PARK
P.O. Box Drawer D
Tahoma, CA 95733
(916) 541-3030

This 593-acre park lies to the south of D.L. Bliss State Park and features a castle and a large waterfall. The view of the lake from atop Eagle Falls is spectacular.

Recommended Ages
Good to Excellent for all ages.

Location
The park is twenty-two miles south of Tahoe City on State Route 89.

Camping Facilities
Two campgrounds, Upper and Lower Eagle Point, in this park have 100 developed sites. Just outside the park is a U.S. Forest Service campground, Bayview. Both campgrounds within the park are near the water, but the sites at Lower Eagle Point offer the best access. On the opposite side of the bay from the campgrounds are twenty primitive campsites for hikers and boaters.

The two developed campgrounds accommodate twenty-one-foot trailers and motor homes, and showers are scattered throughout the campground.

The park is open and on the State Park Reservation System from mid-June to mid-September.

Hiking Activities
The two favorite hikes in this park are the hikes down to Vikingsholm, a replica of a Norse fortress, and the one up to Eagle Falls. Another good hike is from Vikingsholm along the Rubicon Trail to Emerald Point to the north.

All of these originate at the Emerald Bay Overlook along State Route 89 above Emerald Bay. The hike to Vikingsholm is about a mile downhill, and from there it is about a half-mile back up Eagle Creek to the falls. Along the Rubicon Trail from Vikingsholm it is about two miles to Emerald Point.

All of these hikes can be successfully undertaken by strong preschoolers, and they are especially enjoyable for older kids.

Special Outings and Activities

Swimming is enjoyed at a beach below Lower Eagle Point Campground and off the beach and pier near Vikingsholm. Fishing is okay along the lake's shore and off the pier.

FOLSOM LAKE STATE RECREATION AREA

7806 Folsom-Auburn Road
Folsom, CA 95630
(916) 988-0205

This recreation area is a popular water sports area for families who live in the Central Valley. With plenty of beaches, large expanses of water for waterskiing, and good to excellent fishing, this is a great place to head in the hot summer months.

The area also has a number of hike-in campgrounds where you can introduce young children to backpacking.

Recommended Ages

Good for toddlers and preschoolers, Excellent for 6–9 and for 10 and over.

Location

Folsom Lake and the surrounding recreation area are located in the Sierra Foothills twenty-five miles east of Sacramento. The more popular areas around the lake are accessible from I-80 to the east of Roseville.

Camping Facilities

There are three developed and twelve environmental campgrounds at this large recreation area. The most popular campground is the forty-eight-site Beals Point Campground. It has solar-heated showers, is close to the major beach area along the lake, and is near the park entrance along Folsom-Auburn Road. It accommodates thirty-one-foot trailers and motor homes.

Negro Bar Campground is at the upper end of the Lake Natoma, a holding bay below Folsom Dam, and is therefore some distance from the main body of water in the recreation area, Folsom Lake. Its twenty developed sites offer cold showers and accommodate thirty-one-foot trailers and motor homes.

I prefer the more isolated and less developed 100-site Peninsula Campground. It sits beside the lake, off about six miles of dirt road between the two arms of the North and South Forks of the American River. Although there are no showers here, there is great access to the beach, and much less in-and-out traffic by noncampers.

All these campgrounds are open year-round and on the State Park Reservation System from mid-May to mid-September.

Hiking Activities
You can hike almost anywhere along the waterline of the lake, particularly when the level of the lake is down after water is withdrawn for downstream use in the summer.
Along the north shore of the lake the Western States Trail follows the shore. This is a hiking and equestrian trail that leads for over 100 miles from the ridges of the High Sierra down the American River to Nimbus Dam below Folsom Lake. There it joins with the American River Parkway Trail and continues to the confluence of the American and Sacramento rivers near Old Town Sacramento.

Several environmental campgrounds are located along the stretch of trail that runs through the recreation area. Kids will love these easy backpack hikes during the spring and fall. During midsummer the temperatures are just too high most of the time for any sort of backpacking.

Special Outings and Activities
Boating, swimming, fishing, waterskiing, Jet Skiing—you

name a water sport and you can enjoy it at Folsom! However, thousands of people do the same every day during the hot Sacramento summers. That makes for crowded campgrounds, but happy children.

The fishing here is some of the best in the state, and everyone from the youngest to the oldest can enjoy trying their luck, hoping to catch everything from catfish to trout, although bass and perch are the most commonly caught fish.

KLAMATH NATIONAL FOREST
Forest Supervisor
1312 Fairlane Road
Yreka, CA 96097
(916) 842-6131

The Salmon, Scott, and Klamath rivers rush out of the valleys and rugged canyons of half-a-dozen small mountain ranges that are found within the boundaries of this national forest. Most of the campgrounds in the 1,695,000-acre national forest are located along the rivers. The Klamath offers some kayaking and rafting, but fishing is the major sport here. Some of the best salmon and steelhead fishing in California is found along these rivers.

While the Trinity Alps, Russian, Marble Mountain, and Siskiyou wilderness areas pull large numbers of backpackers each year, many of the campgrounds in the forest are lightly used other than during fishing season.

The six ranger districts in the forest all have excellent family campgrounds.

Recommended Ages
Good to Excellent for all ages.

Location
The forest lies along the Oregon border between Eureka and Weed. State Route 96 from Willow Creek to I-5 to the east bisects the northern portion of the forest and several lesser routes cross the southern portion.

Camping Facilities

The twenty-six campgrounds within this national forest are generally small and offer few amenities in comparison with many of the other campgrounds in this guide. What they lack in amenities they more than make up for with their settings.

My favorite campgrounds here are all small, less than twenty-five sites, and offer families a chance to get away from crowds and truly enjoy the outdoors by hiking, swimming, fishing, and loafing.

A good example of these small campgrounds is Idlewild, with twenty-three sites, which sits on the North Fork of the Salmon River and offers great fishing in cold, clear water. On days when the midday heat is just too much the cold water invites the young and brave. When the temperatures are mild this is great hiking country. Several trails lead out from the campground area into the Marble Mountains, one of the most scenic wilderness areas in the country.

Another good, small campground in this national forest is the twenty-three-site Juanita Lake Campground. This lake lies at a 5,100-foot elevation in Butte Valley. While many of the smaller campgrounds in this national forest are not appropriate for families with toddlers and preschoolers, this age group can find much to do at this campground.

It's hard to find a high-altitude lake (6,000 feet and above) that is easily accessible by car, but Kangaroo Lake near the small community of Callahan is one. And a real jewel it is! With only eleven campsites, you'll never find a crowd here. The campground is near a beach, a hiking trail, and trout fishing. It is also a trailhead for the Pacific Crest Trail.

There are plenty of other small campgrounds in this national forest, but many of them have no piped water, a necessity for families with small children. Some do have streams and lakes from which you can filter water, but this is generally too much to do with toddlers and preschoolers.

The higher camps here offer a respite from the hot summers of the lower altitudes, but are generally closed between October and May because of deep snow.

The best way to determine just where you want to camp in this large and wild national forest is to contact the head-quarters and request a map of the forest. All the campgrounds maintained by the national forest are listed, and all roads maintained by the forest service that lead to the more isolated campgrounds are marked.

Hiking Activities

Every campground in the national forests has trails that lead into wild country where you will find solitude away from the crowds around the reservoirs and more popular camp-grounds. These wilderness areas provide hiking opportuni-ties for everyone in the family, from advanced toddlers to grandparents.

Many of the trails into wilderness areas lead to scenic loca-tions, and the trails into the Marble Mountain Wilderness Area are some of the best. Others lead out from just about every campground, and you can go for as far as you want before heading back to the campgrounds.

Special Outings and Activities

People come to this national forest to enjoy high alpine lakes, large reservoirs, and fast-flowing streams and rivers. Whether you like boating, fishing, swimming, or water skiing there is something for you to do.

You don't have to participate in one of these activities to enjoy the lakes and streams here, however, and many peo-ple camp beside the water just to enjoy the magic of waking to the sun reflecting off the still water, watching the afternoon winds whipping up small waves on the open water, and walking along the water's edge at dusk as the sun sets behind the mountains.

LASSEN NATIONAL FOREST
Forest Supervisor
55 South Sacramento Street
Susanville, CA 96130

(916) 257-2151

This 1.2-million-acre national forest extends from the oak-studded foothills of the eastern side of the Sacramento Valley over the southern Cascades and northern Sierra Nevada to the sagebrush country on the Modoc Plateau. It surrounds the Lassen Volcanic National Park and includes one of the largest manmade lakes in California, as well as the second largest natural lake.

Backpackers head for the three wilderness areas in the forest but campers can find plenty of good sites spread throughout the three ranger districts.

Recommended Ages
Good to Excellent for all ages.

Location
To the east of Red Bluff and Redding along the upper end of the Sierra Nevada. Susanville is located on the eastern boundary of the forest. State Routes 89 and 44 cut through the middle of the forest between Susanville and Redding.

Camping Facilities
The three ranger districts in this national forest operate some forty family campgrounds. While many acres of the forest are located at low elevations where camping is likely to be uncomfortable during hot summers, there are a number of wonderful campgrounds at the higher elevations where you can escape the enervating heat.

One of these is Cave Campground along the banks of Hat Creek, a premier trout fishing stream. The campground lies just on the outskirts of Lassen Volcanic National Park and offers great access to several nearby natural features. The campground is well used during trout season, and families flock there in the summer.

A smaller, more isolated campground that is away from the visiting area of the national park is Crater Lake Campground, which sits on the shore of Crater Lake, a little lake at 6,800 feet about thirty miles north of Susanville on the east side of the Cascades. Children like this campground because its seventeen sites are seldom full, and they have access to the wilderness surrounding the lake right from the campground.

Another seventeen-site campground near a high lake is Rocky Knoll Campground on the shores of Silver Lake. This small lake is north of the much larger Lake Almanor and draws few people compared to the many campgrounds near it.

To the south of Lassen Volcanic National Park is a tiny forest service campground along Mill Creek where you have access a state game refuge, as well as good fishing. This is the Hole-in-the-Ground Campground, and all ages can enjoy the activities here.

For those who like larger, more developed campgrounds one of the best in the forest is the 101-site Almanor Campground. This is the most popular campground in the national forest, and it offers great amenities, as well as access to Lake Almanor's excellent fishing.

Hiking Activities

Trails lead from campgrounds in the forest to scenic backcountry that is little changed from when Native Americans roamed the ridges and canyons. There you hike in areas such as the Thousand Lakes Wilderness Area, where you can rest beside small mountain lakes and slow-moving streams.

While many families like to use their campground as a base camp for short backpacking trips, you can decide whether you want to make overnight treks, or simply take long and short day hikes.

Special Outings and Activities

Lassen National Forest covers large regions of ancient and recent volcanic activity, and many of the special activities in the forest are associated with remnants of those geological actions. From exploring lava caves left from ancient lava flows to hiking around boiling lakes to soaking in hot springs, families can enjoy the constant reminders of our ever-changing planet. Fly fishing, boating, and wildlife viewing command attention for others.

Water draws still others to the region to enjoy the magic of watching the rising sun reflect off still waters and listening to the scolding of jays and chicory squirrels before the sun warms the air of mountain mornings.

Children like to explore along the water's edge, search for aquatic animals, and maybe surprise beavers gnawing on alder and aspen along the edge of a meadow.

LASSEN VOLCANIC NATIONAL PARK
P.O. Box 100
Mineral, CA 96063-0100
(916) 595-4444

Recent volcanic activity (recent in geological terms) is the main feature of this seldom visited national park. Huge lava flows, steaming sulfur vents, bubbling mud pots, and boiling lakes reflect the violent activity that is ongoing beneath the surface of the park, and several trails lead to geologic sites.There is much more to the park, however, and over 150 miles of marked trails lead into the beautiful backcountry.

Recommended Ages
Excellent for all ages.

Location
The park is in the southern Cascades between Redding and Susanville. You can reach the park along State Route 32 from Chico, State Route 36 from Red Bluff or State Route 44 from Redding to the west, and State Routes 36 and 44 from Susanville to the east.

Camping Facilities
By far the most popular family campground in the park is Manzanita Lake Campground near the west entrance of the park. This is certainly not a campground where you get away

Even youngsters like to take a break for photography when fantastic views such as this one in Lassen Volcanic National Park stretch out to the horizon.

from it all, however: It has 179 sites that handle trailers and motor homes up to thirty-five feet. There are also all the amenities including a store, gas station, and Laundromat.

Other popular campgrounds in the park include Summit Lake Campground (north and south units) in the middle of the park with ninety-four sites, and Butte Lake Campground in the eastern portion of the park with ninety-eight sites.

Manzanita Lake and Summit Lake campgrounds are centrally located and near the major attractions in the park. Butte Lake Campground is far from the major attractions, although Butte Lake and the nearby cinder cone have plenty to offer campers.

My favorite campground in the park, though, is the smaller and more intimate Warner Valley Campground in the southern portion of the park. This eighteen-site campground doesn't get the steady influx of visitors the larger ones do and is far from the center of activity. Yet, it has plenty of attractions nearby, from the Devil's Kitchen Geothermal Area to a boiling lake. There is also excellent fishing and hiking nearby.

Hiking Activities

Hikes here lead to geologic sites where you can explore and learn before heading back. Short hikes such as the boardwalk at the Sulfur Works are great for even toddlers and preschoolers, while longer hikes such as the one to the top of the cinder cone near Butte Lake require plenty of stamina and perseverance.

One of the most popular hikes in the park, and one that even preschoolers can make, is the two-mile hike down into Bumpass Hell, where a boardwalk leads through mud pots, fumaroles, and small geysers. All children seem to enjoy this display of geologic power, but younger ones are sometimes scared of the hissing and steam that emanates from the openings that lead down to ongoing geothermal activity.

For a good backcountry hike for the older children continue past Bumpass Hell for another mile or so to Boiling Lake, which is also a short hike from the Warner Valley Campground.

Other long trails lead through wild backcountry, and you can backpack in and stay overnight if you obtain a permit from the rangers. If you're adventurous, try the climb to the top of Lassen Peak. This is a strenuous climb but even strong preschoolers who like to hike can make it if everyone is allowed plenty of break time on the way up. If that sounds like a bit much for you, try the level and easy nature trail around Manzanita Lake.

Special Outings and Activities

Most families spend a lot of time driving around Lassen looking at the geologic wonders. Among these are a lava cave and tunnel, a rock slide area beneath Chaos Crags, an area on the northeast side of the slope that was devastated in the last eruption in 1914–17 that is only now beginning to revegetate itself, and the cinder cone and lava fields at Butte Lake. Others prefer to camp at Manzanita Lake and just enjoy the tubing and fishing in this calm lake.

Rangers give campfire talks every night during the summer, and children can participate in Junior Ranger activities during the day. Rangers also lead hikes during the day for adults and children.

LAVA BEDS NATIONAL MONUMENT
P.O. Box 867
Tulelake, CA 96134
(916) 667-2282

The 46,821 acres in this park are dominated by the rugged landscape of lava flows and cinder cones. What vegetation that does grow here is primarily sagebrush and juniper. Within the lava flows explorers have discovered almost 200 lava tube caves of varying sizes, and 21 of these are officially open to the public without permits.

This land of little water and abundant hideaways was the stronghold of the last Native American tribe to hold out against the U.S. Army. In the late 1800s Captain Jack, Chief of the Modocs, fought the final fight of the Modoc War in the northern portion of the monument.

Recommended Ages
Poor for toddlers and preschoolers, Good to Excellent for 6–9 and for 10 and over.

Location
State Route 139 leads through the park and it joins U.S. 395 five miles south of Tulelake and twenty-six miles north of Canby.

Camping Facilities
The forty-site Indian Wells Campground is the only developed campground in this large national monument. During the summer season from Memorial Day to Labor Day the campground has flush toilets and running water, but during the winter months it only has primitive services with no water.

Backcountry camping is allowed within the monument, but only with permits, which can be obtained from monument headquarters. Be aware that there is no dependable supply of water in the backcountry so you must carry all you need—and that can be plenty during midsummer when the temperatures frequently go above 100 degrees.

Hiking Activities

For young children a great hike is the self-guided one around Captain Jack's Stronghold. Here a small band of Modoc Indians held off a large number of U.S. soldiers for a long period during a short-lived war in the last Indian battle in this country.

The hike leads through lava tunnels, Indian hiding places, and to the lone water hole in the area. The cavalry eventually defeated the Modoc warriors by protecting the water hole.

Longer hikes lead into the rugged lava flows where you can find ice caves, lava chimneys, and other formations that children love to explore.

Special Outings and Activities

The really special activity here is the exploration of lava caves. Twenty-one of these are officially open and lights are available at the visitor center if you do not have your own. Rangers can give you directions to these caves and tell you which ones are appropriate for the ages of your children.

MALAKOFF DIGGINS STATE HISTORIC PARK
23579 North Bloomfield Road
Nevada City, CA 95959
(916) 265-2740

This 2,700-acre park showcases the remains of the largest hydraulic gold mine that operated during the last days of the Gold Rush.

Visitors can explore the rugged badlands carved by strong surges of water shot from large water cannons, examine the opening of the 7,847-foot tunnel drilled through bedrock that served as the drain for the slurry formed as the cliffs washed away, or hike on trails first used by gold miners over a century ago.

Families can use pans rented at the park headquarters and museum to try their hands at finding at least some color (small amounts of gold dust found in the sand from creeks and rivers) in the nearby Yuba River.

Recommended Ages
Excellent for all ages.

Location
The park is sixteen miles northeast of Nevada City on North Bloomfield Road.

Camping Facilities
The Short Hill Campground here has thirty developed sites and accommodates eighteen-foot trailers and twenty-four-foot motor homes. The campground lies a short, easy walk from the historic town of North Bloomfield, where the park service also rents two rustic cabins. The waiting list for these is generally long, but you may be lucky and find one vacant on your visit. Children like to sleep on the hard bunks and cook on the woodstove that is the sole source of heat in each cabin. There are also several environmental campsites for those who wish to walk in a way to get away from other campers.

The campground is open year-round and on the State Park Reservation System from May to mid-September.

Hiking Activities
Several short trails, Marton Ranch, Upper Humbug, Church, North Bloomfield, and Slaughterhouse, begin near the park headquarters in the historical area of the park and lead to the campground, Blair Lake, and the beginning of Diggins Loop Trail. All of these short trails are easy and even preschoolers enjoy hiking them.

A little longer hike is the Diggins Loop Trail that takes you around the Diggins Pond where the last hydraulic mining was done in the park. This trail leads you through badlands that were formed by hydraulic pumps rather than by thousands of years of erosion. Older children like to explore this area where the water from the mining was collected before being poured through a gigantic sluice where the gold was collected.

Across the road from the Diggins Loop trailhead is the trailhead for the Humbug Trail that follows the steps of old miners downhill to the South Fork of the Yuba River. A Bureau of Land Management campground sits beside the river at the end of the trail, and this makes an excellent overnight hike for older kids. A longer, full-day hike leads along the Rim Trail above the park.

Special Outings and Activities

History is the focus of most activities in this park. The mining museum, a blacksmith shop that is occasionally fired up, and gold mining along a creek below the museum with pans rented from the rangers are all close to the park headquarters and the campground.

You may encounter ongoing research in state parks, such as this archaeological excavation at Malakoff Diggins State Park.

Youngsters can swim in the creek (toddlers and preschoolers), in the Yuba River, and at Blair Lake, an old holding pond for supplying water to the hydraulic pumps used in the mining. The lake is deep and the walls are extremely steep, so only those children who are strong swimmers should be allowed to swim there.

There is some fishing for pan fish in the lake, the creek, and the river, but adults will consider the pickings slim.

McARTHUR-BURNEY FALLS MEMORIAL STATE PARK
Route 1, Box 1260
Burney, CA 96013
(916) 335-2777

Burney Falls, a 129-foot waterfall on Burney Creek, is the most spectacular feature of this 768-acre park, but there are plenty of other activities to keep the whole family occupied. The trout fishing nearby is some of the best in the nation, and trails lead through beautiful conifer forests.

Swimming, boating, and other water sports are popular along the banks of Lake Britton, a nine-mile-long, manmade lake adjoining the park.

Recommended Ages
Excellent for all ages.

Location
Head eleven miles north of Burney on State Route 89 to reach the park entrance.

Camping Facilities
Two campgrounds, Pioneer and Rim, in this park have a total of 118 sites. Neither of the campgrounds is close to the lake, where many of the family activities occur, but you can walk along several trails to the water with ease. There are showers scattered throughout the campgrounds, and the sites accommodate thirty-two-foot trailers and forty-five-foot motor homes.

The campgrounds are open and on the State Park Reservation System year-round.

Hiking Activities
Hiking is not a real focus of this park, although a section of the Pacific Crest Trail does wind through the center of it. Other trails lead along Burney Creek, to Burney Falls, and to a headwaters pool upstream from the falls. All of these offer excellent hiking, but only the Burney Creek and Rim trails are appropriate for preschoolers.

A fire road leads up to the old pioneer cemetery, and many people hike up it from the campgrounds.

Special Outings and Activities
Swimming and fishing are extremely popular activities here, and both are good to excellent. The lake is stocked with trout early in the summer, and the beaches gently slope into the water so even toddlers can play along the edges. They can also find shallow pools in the creek where they can play and look for aquatic creatures. Boating and associated water sports are very popular in the lake, and there is a boat launch in the park, along with boat and water ski rentals.

The falls attract a lot of attention, and some people just like to sit and watch them cascade over the rocks.

Rangers give campfire talks every night in the summer, and lead hikes for adults and children during the day. Children can also participate in Junior Ranger activities.

The McArthur-Burney Heritage Days, a celebration of the early settlers in the region, are held in mid-October each year at the park. These are living history days with displays and activities from the mid- to late 1800s, open to all.

MENDOCINO NATIONAL FOREST
Forest Supervisor
420 East Laurel Street
Willows, CA 95988
(916) 934-3316

This sixty-five-mile-long, thirty-five-mile-wide national forest lies to the east of U.S. 101 in northwestern California. Over half of the forest is covered with mixed stands of ponderosa pine, sugar pine, Douglas fir, and incense cedar. Wildlife is abundant in here, with an estimated 20,000 blacktail deer and 350 black bear living in the mountainous terrain. The forest has two wilderness areas and four ranger districts.

Recommended Ages
Good to Excellent for all ages.

Location
Along the Coast Range between redwood country and the Central Valley. Access from I-5 to the east is limited to unimproved forest service roads from small towns such as Stonyford, Elk Creek, and Paskenta. Access from U.S. 101 leads through Covelo and Garberville.

Camping Facilities
Most of the thirty campgrounds in this national forest are small or tiny, but that only adds to their allure for me. I like to search out a small, developed campground that is lightly used and spend a week or so just lying back and relaxing.

One such campground in the Mendocino National Forest is located at Hammerhorn Lake, which sits at the 3,500-foot level northeast of Covelo. As with most of the campgrounds in the forest, summers can get very warm, some would even say very hot, and five-acre Hammerhorn offers water to cool off the body and soul.

There are only eight sites that accommodate trailers and motor homes here, but the seclusion one finds along the shores of the small lake is enough to satisfy my search for great campgrounds.

At a little higher elevation (6,500 feet), and a little larger with twenty-five sites, the Wells Cabin campground is another great find. During the summer few people venture this far into the wilderness to camp, but the sites accommodate trailers and motor homes to twenty-two feet. While there is no lake or stream nearby, there is plenty of hiking available from the campground.

Two lakes on the east side of the forest that are lightly used and have good campgrounds are Plaskett and Letts. Plaskett is actually two small lakes that are nestled among a conifer forest at the 6,000-foot elevation, and a little-known campground nearby is Plaskett Meadows. With thirty-two sites, this secluded campground seldom fills up, yet the views of Black Butte Mountain are worth the trials and tribulations one must undertake to reach the campground.

Letts Lake is south of Plaskett Meadows at 4,500 feet, and few people seem to know about this thirty-five-acre jewel where no motorboats are allowed. This makes it an ideal place to take young children to learn about canoeing, rafting, tubing, fishing, and swimming, all of which are excellent on the still waters. The forty-two sites in the campground are spread around the shore of the lake and are secluded from each other. They accommodate motor homes and trailers to twenty feet.

On the west side of the forest, and north of Clear Lake, lies Lake Pillsbury. This reservoir is a popular fishing and camping spot, and the forest service operates ten campgrounds to serve the many visitors who come for the fishing, boating, and water sports. These campgrounds range in size from the fifty-four-site Sunset Campground to the six-site Lower Nye Campground. Most of these fill up on summer weekends and major holiday weeks, but you can generally find a site in one of them if you come early on a Friday or anytime during the early part of the week.

Hiking Activities
This national forest lies at a lower altitude than many in Northern California, and summers are consequently hotter. This makes hiking less than desirable during midsummer. Moderate fall and spring weather makes great times to ven-

ture into the wilder regions of the forest where humans have left few marks even after centuries of exploration.

Short hikes near the campgrounds are good year-round. Longer hikes such as those into the Snow Mountain Wilderness Area are great during the cooler months before and after the heavy winter rains that lash the region.

Special Outings and Activities
Lake Pillsbury, the only large body of water in this forest, attracts families who like to participate in water sports such as motor boating, fishing, and water skiing. Those who like their quiet and solitude head into campgrounds farther away from civilization. There they find little water, except in spring after heavy winter rains, but plenty of wildlife such as deer, rabbit, coyote, and a wide variety of birds.

MODOC NATIONAL FOREST
Forest Supervisor
441 North Main Street, P.O. Box 611
Alturas, CA 96101
(916) 233-5811

Almost 2 million acres are included in this forest in the northeast corner of California. Rugged obsidian mountains, lava caves, and volcanic craters are found along the western boundary of the forest, and to the east the Warner Mountains offer crystal clear mountain lakes, plenty of cold mountain streams, and great fishing along the upper reaches of the Pit River.

Each of the four ranger districts in the forest have outstanding campgrounds where you can fish, hike, and swim in cold waters.

Recommended Ages
Good to Excellent for all ages.

Location
This large national forest lies to the southeast of Tulelake on

the lightly populated Modoc Plateau and is split south to north by U.S. 395.

Camping Facilities

For so large a national forest there are relatively few campgrounds, only nineteen, and none of those have as many as fifty sites. This makes camping in the region a joyful experience if you are looking for a spot to get away from it all.

I generally head for the Warner Mountain Ranger District in this forest, although there are two campgrounds in the Doublehead and Big Valley ranger districts that I like. Let me describe them first. The twin, twenty-two-site Medicine Lake and A.H. Hogue campgrounds are just south of the Lava Beds National Monument. These campgrounds surround Medicine Lake, which sits in an old volcano in the midst of sugar pine and fir trees.

There are three other national forest campgrounds around the lake, but the first two are my favorites. More secluded campgrounds are the Upper and Lower Rush Creek campgrounds farther to the south in the Big Valley Ranger District where the forests are denser. These two tiny campgrounds, one has thirteen sites and the other eight, are located beside a cool mountain stream in a steep canyon. Even on holiday weekends such as Memorial Day and the Fourth of July, when everywhere else is full, you are still likely to find a spot here.

It is the Warner Mountain area that attracts me, though, for few people other than hunters and fishermen venture into this lonely range. That's good for me and you, if you like beautiful scenery, cool summers, good fishing and hiking, and few people when you head for a campground. Mill Creek Falls Campground, with nineteen sites, is only one of about a dozen campgrounds in the region where you can camp among tall trees, walk along cool streams, and climb up scenic mountains with eye-catching rock outcroppings and geological formations at every turn in the trail.

Other favorites there include the forty-eight-site Blue Lake

Campground and the six-site Cave Lake Campground. Of these Blue Lake is most likely to fill up because Cave Lake is hard to reach even for those seeking secluded sites to spend a quiet vacation.

Hiking Activities
Trails in this large national forest don't lead into heavily forested terrain where you can seek refuge from the noonday sun, but along open ridges and across sage-covered plains. While this makes midsummer hiking difficult as temperatures rise, it makes hiking interesting when they are milder. Scenic vistas, herds of pronghorn and deer, abundant birdlife, and coyotes that seem to speak to the world during moonlit nights all become part of your world as you hike during early morning or late evenings.

Open trails lead out from all the campgrounds in the forest, and you can hike as far as you like. If you decide to spend a night in the backcountry make sure you carry plenty of water, which is scarce in this region.

Special Outings and Activities
Unlike many national forests in Northern California, water is not a big draw in Modoc. Water is a precious commodity here, and that makes wildlife viewing much easier than in many regions. With few dependable sources of water, animals tend to congregate around the few areas where water is available year-round. That makes it easier to view large numbers of larger mammals such as deer and pronghorn, and setting up camp near a watering hole makes it easy to sneak up on watering herds.

Birds are another reason to visit this forest, and you can see large flocks of ducks and geese during both the fall migration and the spring mating season. Grouse are also plentiful in the sage brush-covered land, and you can hear their mating calls during the spring as you hike in the morning or evening.

PLUMAS EUREKA STATE PARK
310 Johnsville Road
Blairsden, CA 96103
(916) 836-2380

This park, which sits high in the Sierra in Plumas County, offers both natural and human history in an almost perfect blend. The park museum, partially restored stamp mill, and nearby historic Johnsville all portray the region as it was during the heady days in the last half of the 1800s when the lure of gold brought thousands of miners to this idyllic site about fifty miles north of Lake Tahoe off State Route 89.

The granite peaks, beautiful lakes, serene meadows, and quiet streams in and near the park offer exceptionally scenic destinations for those campers who wish to hike along mountain trails.

Even those who don't want to venture far from the campground can choose among a variety of nature activities. These include climbing on nearby rocks and enjoying water activities at Jamison Creek, which flows through the campground.

Recommended Ages
Excellent for all ages.

Location
Plumas Eureka State Park is located about fifty miles north of Lake Tahoe off State Route 89. At Graeagle take County Road A14 west from State Route 89 for five miles to the park entrance.

The park sits in a fir, pine, and cedar forest between 4,720 and 7,447 feet. U.S. Forest Service land surrounds the park, and trails from the park lead to a number of beautiful mountain lakes on national forest land.

Camping Facilities
There are sixty-seven campsites in the campground nestled in a forested canyon along both sides of Jamison Creek. All campsites have tables, stove pits, and food lockers. Piped

water and combination showers/restrooms are scattered among the campsites.

The campground is open on a first-come, first-served basis between May 1 and October 15 each year. The campground fills quickly on weekends between Memorial Day and Labor Day. The best days to reach the park are Sunday afternoons and early in the week.

There are about a dozen tent-only sites, and about twenty-five that will accept RVs and trailers over thirty feet.

My favorite sites are on the west side of Jamison Creek as you enter the campground. These offer good access to the creek, and several sites have excellent climbing rocks nearby.

Hiking Activities

There are three moderate marked trails within the park itself, plus a short trail from the campground to the Jamison Mine site that is less than a quarter mile long.

The Campground/Museum Trail is approximately 1.5 miles long and leads through a mixed pine–fir forest to the museum. This is an easy hike for even young children (those three and above can make it easily). If you wish, one adult can take a car to the museum to drive everyone back to the campground. Part of this trail is included in a self-guided nature trail that loops back to the trailhead.

The Madora Loop trail is a 1.5-mile loop around serene Lake Madora. The parking lot for this hike is located off County Road A14. The hike is especially beautiful in early summer when the wildflowers are in full bloom, but is interesting anytime. You may see osprey that nest in the top of a snag in the lake, and an occasional bald eagle has been spotted flying over the lake. This hike is level and enjoyable even for toddlers if you take your time.

The Eureka Peak Loop Trail is for those who want to stretch their legs a bit. To reach the trailhead you drive up a fire road to the dam at Eureka Lake. From there you take the three-mile loop trail that leads by 7,447-foot Eureka Peak and the lower North Peak. From both you have panoramic views of

Backcountry hikes in the Sierra and Cascades frequently lead to beaver ponds like this one in Plumas Eureka State Park.

the Sierra Nevada that include Lassen Peak to the north.

Other hikes can be made into the national forest by taking the trail to Jamison Mine. From there a trail leads along Upper Jamison Creek to Grass, Rock, Jamison, and Wades lakes. It is 1.8 miles to Grass Lake from Jamison Mine. It is another 1.5 miles to the other lakes. There is an active beaver colony at Grass Lake, and Rock Lake is one of the bluest lakes you will ever see. About a mile from Jamison Mine, before you reach Grass Lake, a trail leads off to the right to Smith Lake, which is another mile along the trail.

The hikes to these lakes are moderate, and any children over six should be able to make them with a little stopping along the trail. Each of the lakes offers something slightly different, but all are cold mountain lakes that only the intrepid dare swim in.

Hikes to the lakes are good day outings. You might, however, want to take your sleeping bags and make an overnight trip to one of them. If you plan to hike in overnight you must first obtain a fire permit from the USFS station in Blairsden.

Special Outings and Activities
A great feature of this park is the historical section where
everyone can learn more about the Gold Rush days. Short
hikes from the visitor center and museum take you to a partially restored stamp mill, a working blacksmith shop, and
downtown Johnsville, where you can walk to the old cemetery.

Although the fishing is not outstanding, you can cast into
the waters of Jamison Creek, the cold mountain lakes above
the park in the national forest, and Lake Madora.

Kids who are old enough to swim like to head for the
swimming hole on Jamison Creek below the cemetery. Follow the unmarked, but well-traveled trail down a steep grade
to the creek. There is a ten-foot-high waterfall that rushes into
a good-sized pool that is about ten to twelve feet deep at the
deepest part, but shallow enough around the edges for nonswimmers to enjoy. You can also explore along the creek above
the falls, where there are ponds for you to soak in the cold
water on hot days.

For younger children there are a number of small, shallow
water holes along both Jamison and Upper Jamison Creek
in and near the campground where they can play. For those
who like a little warmer water for swimming a short drive
to the Old Mill Pond in nearby Graeagle is a delightful outing on warm days.

PLUMAS NATIONAL FOREST
Forest Supervisor
159 Lawrence Street, P.O. Box 11500
Quincy, CA 95971-6025

This 1,146,900-acre national forest lies at the junction of the
Cascade and Sierra Nevada ranges in northern California. The
mountainous terrain includes nearly all of the Feather River
drainage, and much of the area is extremely steep.

The Middle Fork of the Feather River is part of the National
Wild and Scenic River System, and the sixth highest waterfall in the country, Feather Falls, is located in the national for-

est. Another popular area in the forest is Lakes Basin, where over fifty lakes dot a landscape of exposed granite. This area is popular with hikers and backpackers.

The forest has one wilderness area and six ranger districts.

Recommended Ages
Good to Excellent for all ages.

Location
The national forest lies between Lake Tahoe and Lassen Volcanic National Park in the Sierra Nevada. State Routes 89 and 70 cut through the forest and many smaller, less-improved roads lead into the campgrounds from these two main routes.

Camping Facilities
Although it has only about half the acreage of Modoc National Forest to the north, Plumas has several dozen more campgrounds that attract families during the warm summer months.

Many of these campgrounds are located along the shores of small reservoirs such as Bucks Lake and Little Grass Valley Reservoir, or around the massive Lake Oroville. Around Bucks Lake, I favor Mill Creek (ten sites) and Whitehorse (twenty sites) campgrounds where you are near the lake and hiking trails. At Little Grass Valley I always try to get a site at Wyandotte Campground, which has thirty-two sites on a peninsula that juts into the reservoir.

About seven miles from Bucks Lake is Silver Lake, where a seven-site campground almost always has at least one open site. Most people who venture into Bucks seem not to know about this seldom visited, but exquisite, lake.

A more popular spot in the national forest is Antelope Lake at 5,000 feet elevation to the south of Plumas Eureka State Park. There three campgrounds that range in size from thirty-eight to eighty-six sites surround the lake, and all have good access to the water.

Hiking Activities

Plumas National Forest is heavily wooded and has rugged terrain and dozens of small reservoirs along fast-flowing rivers. This makes for strenuous but enjoyable hiking. Most campgrounds have three or four trails leading into the surrounding wilderness, and families can find new adventures each day. Water is plentiful near most campgrounds, and you can take frequent breaks near lakes or streams as you hike.

Special Outings and Activities

Fishing in cold mountain streams, boating on small reservoirs, and swimming on hot summer days are all popular activities in this national forest.

Even if you don't participate in these water sports, you can still enjoy the many lakes and streams. Wake early before the sun peaks over the ridges and watch as the rising sun replaces dark shadows and reflects off the calm water of the lakes. Hike along streams, taking short breaks to watch the water ripple over large rocks in the stream bed. Dip your toes in the cold water as you eat a snack. Stand on the east side of lakes in late afternoon and watch the sun drop behind distant peaks. All of these are great ways to spend your hours while camping in the Plumas National Forest.

SHASTA-TRINITY NATIONAL FORESTS

Forest Supervisor
2400 Washington Avenue
Redding, CA 96001
(916) 246-5222

Smack dab in the middle of northern California are the Shasta and Trinity National Forests. The forests range from low-elevation grass and oak lands to 14,162-foot Mt. Shasta. The forests have five wilderness areas, three major reservoirs, and seven ranger districts in their more than 2 million acres.

Of all the national forest units in California, these two are among the best for recreational opportunities. There are 1,377 miles of trails (150 miles of these are part of the Pacific Crest

Trail), 1,900 miles of fishing streams, 114 named natural lakes, and eleven manmade reservoirs in the forests. Over eighty developed campgrounds provide campers ideal spots to enjoy the many recreational activities in the area.

Recommended Ages
Good to Excellent for all ages.

Location
The forests are located in the central part of northern California between the Coast Range to the west and the Cascades to the east. Interstate 5 bisects the forests north to south and State Route 299 runs along their southern border. State Route 89 runs along the eastern and northern boundaries.

Camping Facilities
There are probably as many campgrounds within the boundaries of these national forests as in all other state and national parks in Northern California, although some of them are heavily used others are seldom full.

Most of the campgrounds are found near the large reservoirs, Whiskeytown, Clair Engle, Lewiston, and Shasta lakes. The campgrounds at Whiskeytown are operated by the National Park Service, but the others are operated by the national forests. I must admit that I have never camped at any of this multitude of campgrounds because I simply don't like the crowds of people who come to the lakes for water sports. I am sure there is nothing wrong with any of the camping areas, and some may be excellent. I just can't make any recommendations about them.

I generally come to this region to backpack into the wilderness areas such as the Trinity Alps, Castle Crags, and Mt. Shasta. I have camped in a number of smaller campgrounds away from the large reservoirs as I have prepared for my backpacking trips, and several are very good for families, and not all that crowded.

To the southwest of Hayfork along the North Fork of Salt

Creek is a very special campground. Philpot has only six sites, but for a quiet vacation where you can relax, hike, fish, and soak in the cool water, it can't be beat.

An even smaller campground (three tent sites) is located off State Route 299 along the Trinity River. Seldom do you find such a small campground with piped water, but this is one you won't want to miss if you want to have all the conveniences of a forest service campground, but be all by yourself near a great fishing, hiking, and swimming area.

In the eastern portion of the national forest the vegetation and topography is very different from the river country to the west. Instead of roaring rivers and steep canyons there are gentle streams and rolling country, and there you can find several delightful campgrounds. Ah-Di-Na, Fowlers Camp, McBride Springs, and Toad Lake are all small campgrounds (six to thirty-nine sites) in scenic areas where quiet takes precedence over raucous behavior, and people come for the trout and the wildflowers more than the loud water sports that predominate at the large reservoirs.

Hiking Activities

Hiking is great in this forest. Longer trails lead from several campgrounds into the Trinity Alps, Marble Mountain, Mt. Shasta, and Castle Crags wilderness areas, and shorter trails lead along rivers and streams from almost all campgrounds.

This is rugged country, and longer hikes should be taken only if you are familiar with the trails, either from past trips or by talking with rangers. Always carry plenty of water, or a water purifier, as you head out on longer hikes.

Special Outings and Activities

Fishing in cold mountain streams, swimming in the larger reservoirs, and boating activities are all popular here. Those who don't like water sports can explore around the lakes and streams in search of small wildlife.

The small campgrounds here are a good place to head if you want to take it easy and relax away from crowds.

SUGAR PINE POINT STATE PARK
P.O. Box 266
Tahoma, CA 95733
(916) 525-7982

This large state park is the only state park within the Tahoe Basin that stays open year-round. While the 2,011 acres within the park include beautiful forests and almost two miles of lake frontage, it is also a popular staging area for hikers headed for High Sierra backcountry such as Desolation Valley.

Alpine wildflowers abound in late spring and early summer in the park, and visitors can enjoy the colorful blossoms on short hikes in the park or on longer hikes in the high country nearby.

Recommended Ages
Excellent for all ages.

Location
The park lies along the shore of Lake Tahoe about ten miles south of Tahoe City on State Route 89.

Camping Facilities
The large campground here has 175 developed sites, and they are full all summer. All the sites are across State Route 89 from the half-mile-long beach that draws families during the summer months for swimming and sunbathing. The sites have showers during the summer, and accommodate twenty-four-foot trailers and thirty-foot motor homes.

The campground here is the only one of all the state parks along the shores of Lake Tahoe that stays open year-round, but services are somewhat limited during the winter.

The campground is on the State Park Reservation System from mid-June to mid-September.

Hiking Activities
Hiking here is excellent. Preschoolers like the hike through the nature preserve to the Sugar Pine Point Lighthouse, the

Waterfalls with swimming holes below abound
along the many rivers of the Sierra Nevada.

trail for the handicapped near the interpretive center (toddlers like this one), and the Rod Beaudry Trail from the interpretive center to the campfire center.

Older children like to head up the trail beside General
Creek. There are beautiful wildflower blooms here in the
spring, and hummingbirds collect here in the summer. If you
continue on this trail you head into the Desolation Wilderness Area, one of the most scenic in California with outstanding granite outcroppings and alpine lakes.

Special Outings and Activities
Swimming, fishing, and sunbathing are all favorite activities

in and near the lake, and younger children like to explore along the creek banks as they hike along upstream.

Rangers lead campfire talks nightly, and hikes for adults and children during the day. Older children can join in Junior Ranger activities during the day.

TAHOE NATIONAL FOREST
Forest Supervisor
631 Coyote Street, P.O. Box 6003
Nevada City, CA 95959-6003
(916) 265-4531

This popular national forest offers great scenery with a temperate climate. These make it one of the most popular recreational destinations in the northern Sierra.

The five ranger districts in the forest provide over seventy-five campgrounds for families and groups, with most near rivers, streams, and lakes where everyone can enjoy water activities such as boating, fishing, and swimming.

Recommended Ages
Good to Excellent for all ages.

Location
The forest extends from Lake Tahoe north to the Sierra Buttes.

Camping Facilities
With almost seventy family campgrounds it is hard to even begin to pick out a favorite. These campgrounds are located beside roaring mountain streams, cool rivers, tree-shaded lakes, and reservoirs with excellent fishing.

Isolated Grouse Ridge Campground is located at the end of a lightly used road at 7,400 feet above Lake Spaulding, and with only nine sites is a great place to find solitude.

Sardine and Salmon Creek campgrounds sit in the shadows of the Sierra Buttes, an outstanding volcanic outcropping, and offer warm days and cool nights at 5,800 feet. These lakes offer great swimming and fishing for youngsters, and even toddlers can find a place to play in the water during warm afternoons. These are great for families who want to camp, but don't want to go too far from civilization.

There are literally dozens of other campgrounds in this national forest that offer camping just as good as the ones I have mentioned above. Contact the forest headquarters to find out more about them and ask for a map and any literature they have published on the campgrounds in the forest.

Hiking Activities

As with many national forests in Northern California, hiking is almost unlimited here. Trails lead into unpopulated wilderness, as well as around lakes and along streams near campgrounds. Families with children of all ages can find something that satisfies the needs of everyone near most campgrounds.

For the more adventurous, longer trails lead into the scenic Granite Chief Wilderness Area where bare granite peaks rise above the heavily forested canyons below.

Keep a sharp eye out for small creatures such as this frog.

Special Outings and Activities

Alpine wildflowers are a special treat in many areas of this national forest. If you camp here in June and July you can almost always find a meadow full of delicate wildflowers. If you are new to the region, ask the rangers where you should head for the most colorful displays.

Kids also like to watch for small mammals such as ground squirrels, chipmunks, and tree squirrels as they hike along forest trails.

CHAPTER 5

CENTRAL COAST CAMPING

E lephant seals, Stellar sea lions, and gray whales can all be seen up close along the 350 miles of the central coast that extends from San Francisco south to Ventura.

In the north end of this region large stands of coast redwood are the centerpiece of several state parks near Santa Cruz, and many families head for these as soon as the heavy winter rains pass. These parks are near major population centers, though, and this makes for crowded campgrounds where reservations are essential.

Some of the most beautiful and least spoiled coastline in the state lies along State Route 1 to the south of Monterey. Jagged cliffs rise above pounding surf where occasional isolated beaches offer a place for a midday picnic near the rolling waves.

The rugged wilderness areas of the Big Sur region rise to the east, and there are few roads into the area. Hiking is the only way to explore most of the canyons and ridges there, and even hiking trails are lightly used. This is one place where you can head for solitude and find it.

As you continue south from Big Sur, campgrounds are scattered in pockets along the coast. These become more heavily

Central Coast Camping

KEY TO PARKS

1. *Butano State Park*
2. *Big Basin Redwoods State Park*
3. *Henry Cowell Redwoods State Park*
4. *Los Padres National Forest*
5. *Morro Bay Area State Parks*
6. *Pfeiffer-Big Sur State Park*
7. *Pinnacles National Monument*
8. *Portola State Park*

used as you get closer to the Los Angeles metropolitan area. The warm waters and long sandy beaches are worth any effort it takes to reserve a campsite, however, and trips to them make great late winter and spring outings.

BIG BASIN REDWOODS STATE PARK
Big Basin, CA 95006
(408) 338-6132

This 18,000-acre park is the oldest park in the California State Park System. Large groves of gigantic redwoods are the big attraction in the park, but there area also several waterfalls, including sixty-five-foot-high Berry Falls, and plenty of wildlife to see.

Camping opportunities include developed campsites, walk-in camps, and trail camps for backpackers.

Recommended Ages
Excellent for all ages.

Location
The park lies twenty miles north of Santa Cruz by State Routes 9 and 236.

Camping Facilities
Four campgrounds with 143 developed drive-in sites and 45 developed walk-in sites offer excellent camping in this redwood park. In addition, there are six trail camps for backpackers spread throughout the large park. The developed sites accommodate twenty-seven-foot trailers and thirty-foot motor homes.

You can't miss with any of the campgrounds here, but the farther away from the park headquarters you are the less traffic and noise you will encounter. Huckleberry Campground is the most isolated, while Blooms Creek Campground is nearest the headquarters and most facilities.

The campgrounds are open and on the State Park Reservation System year-round. The campgrounds fill quickly

Redwoods soar above hikers in state parks such as Big Basin and Butano.

during the summer months and reservations are a necessity, but you can frequently find a vacancy in early fall when hiking among the redwoods is at its best.

If you wish to see the waterfalls in full force you should try to camp at the park in early spring after the heaviest of the winter rains have ceased.

Hiking Activities

Hiking is excellent in this park, and there are almost 100 miles of trails to choose from. The trails range from the short Redwood Trail near the park headquarters, which even preschoolers can easily undertake, to the long Skyline-to-the-Sea Trail, which taxes even well-conditioned adults.

The hike to the seventy-foot high Berry Creek Falls takes over two hours, but older children love the trek and enjoy the falls rushing over outcrops of moss-covered rock.

Other trails lead to huge redwoods that tower above seasonal creeks. Younger children like to explore along the banks of these, especially in late spring and early summer when water still flows along the creek beds and thickets of fern cast shadows over the deeper holes.

Special Outings and Activities

A hike to all four major waterfalls in the park makes a great outing, but for families who like more sedentary activities, watching for birds in the tall trees, playing in the shallow water of the seasonal creeks, and driving along the paved roads of the park in search of large trees all are great ways to spend a vacation.

A Junior Ranger program offers plenty of daytime activities for older children, and there are ranger-led hikes for adults, children, and families most days. Rangers lead campfire talks most nights during the summer.

In April each year about 100 people show up at Big Basin to participate in the annual Trail Days sponsored by the Santa Cruz Mountain Trail Association. These people pitch in and help repair old trails and build sections of new ones. This is a great time to plan a weekend camping trip. You can work hard on the trails one day, and hike others the next.

BUTANO STATE PARK
P.O. Box 9
Pescadero, CA 94060
(415) 879-0173

This medium-size (3,200 acre) redwood park is located in an isolated region of the Santa Cruz Mountains. Families come here to enjoy hikes along year-round creeks and on old logging roads to the top of ridges where the views include the Pacific Ocean to the west.

The park has a trail camp for backpackers and many families like to use this for young backpackers before they head out on longer hikes.

Recommended Ages
Poor to Good for toddlers and preschoolers, Excellent for 6–9 and for 10 and over.

Location

The park lies about halfway between Santa Cruz and Half Moon Bay on Cloverdale Road about five miles south of the small community of Pescadero.

Camping Facilities

For those who want to avoid the large number of campers who head for the more popular state parks in this region, this park is a good place to head. There are only twenty-one developed drive-in sites in the park, plus nineteen developed walk-in ones. There is also a trail camp for backpackers.

The campground has most amenities, but no showers, and the sites accommodate twenty-four-foot trailers and twenty-seven-foot motor homes.

The drive-in sites are open and on the State Park Reservation System year-round. The walk-in sites are open all year, but only on the State Park Reservation System from April through September.

Hiking Activities

A number of hiking trails and fire roads in the park offer excellent outings for both young and old. Except for several short trails near the campground, which preschoolers and even advanced toddlers can enjoy, most of the trails in this park involve steep climbs over rugged terrain.

The longer trails lead along creeks, up steep slopes, and along the top of ridges where many good stops for a midday snack are located. From one of these you can view Ano Nuevo Island and the ocean to the west.

Special Outings and Activities

There are few special events and outings in this secluded park. You have to make your own if you want more than the chance to relax and hike through forests of tall redwoods.

For younger children, Butano Creek offers a great place to explore and even a chance to drop a fishing line in running water. Fishing isn't great, and may be limited during spawning seasons, but the kids love it. There are ranger-led hikes on some days, and some summer nights rangers lead campfire talks.

You can make a backpack trip into the Butano Trail camp a special treat for older children, but you must arrange this with the rangers before you head out.

HENRY COWELL REDWOODS STATE PARK
101 North Big Trees Park Road
Felton, CA 95018
(408) 335-4598

Some of the largest redwoods in Santa Cruz County are found in this 4,082-acre park. Over fifteen miles of hiking trails lead through these fantastic groves and along the San Lorenzo River. From November to February the river is open to steelhead and silver salmon fishing, and during the summer families enjoy swimming in deep holes in the river.

Recommended Ages
Poor to Good for toddlers and preschoolers, Excellent for 6–9 and for 10 and over.

Location
The park is five miles north of Santa Cruz on State Route 9.

Camping Facilities
The 113-site campground at this park is some distance from the park headquarters and day use area and has a separate entrance off Graham Hill Road. The sites accommodate twenty-seven-foot trailers and thirty-five-foot motor homes and have all the amenities, including hot showers that are placed throughout the campground.

The campground is open throughout the year and on the State Park Reservation System between April and October.

Hiking Activities
Although there are only about fifteen miles of hiking trails

within the boundaries of the park, there is a good hike for just about everyone. Trails take you to an observation deck with great views of Santa Cruz to the west, to Big Rock Hole along the San Lorenzo River, to Cathedral Redwood where a ring of tall redwoods grow from a single stump of what was once a gigantic tree, along the river where you can find both deep and shallow holes for children to play in and around, and to a redwood grove along a nature trail near the headquarters.

While some of these trails require considerable stamina, others, such as the River and Nature Trails, are relatively level and even toddlers and preschoolers can enjoy them.

Special Outings and Activities

During midsummer kids like to play in the San Lorenzo River, where the older ones can find deep holes to dive into and the younger ones can wade in shallow waters as they search for aquatic animals.

Fishing is good to excellent here during steelhead and silver salmon fishing season between mid-November and the end of February. The river is closed to any kind of fishing the rest of the year.

There is a small museum and nature exhibit area at the park headquarters, and youngsters can learn about the active Junior Ranger program there. Rangers also lead hikes during the day for adults, children, and families. At night during the busy summer season the rangers give campfire talks at the campground.

About ten miles of trail are designated for horseback riding, but there are no campsites with pens to hold horses for equestrians who wish to spend several days in the park.

This park is a great place to head in midwinter to hunt for mushrooms, and the Santa Cruz Museum of Natural History holds a fungus fair each January to introduce novices to the more than 150 species of fungi that flourish in the wooded areas of Santa Cruz County.

The park also hosts Ohlone Days in late September where

the whole family can learn about how Native Americans lived in the region before the invasion of the Europeans.

On Halloween each year the park staff dresses up as make-believe forest creatures and entertains children between the ages of four and eleven for a night of fun.

LOS PADRES NATIONAL FOREST
Forest Supervisor
6144 Calle Road
Goleta, CA 93117
(805) 683-6711

This is the third largest national forest in California with almost 2 million acres. It is divided into two sections along the central coast, with the largest section extending inland from Santa Barbara.

This is one of only three national forests in the U.S. with ocean frontage, and it is a land of great contrasts. Inland day-time temperatures can reach well over 100 degrees and the chaparral that covers the steep terrain becomes tinder for

Harbor seals use off-shore rocks as haul-out sites all along the central coast.

wildfires that make this one of the most burned forests in the nation. The forest has five wilderness areas and five ranger districts with over 1,500 miles of marked trails and over seventy developed campgrounds.

While much of the forest is located in the Santa Barbara area, the Monterey Ranger District lies to the east of State Route 1 just south of Carmel along the Big Sur coast and includes the Santa Lucia Mountains.

Recommended Ages
Good to Excellent for all ages.

Location
The forest extends into six counties along the central coast from Ventura almost to Carmel and inland as far as I-5.

Camping Facilities
Camping is plentiful in this national forest, and campers can enjoy this park all year since the climate is temperate throughout the year. During the summer months the temperatures reach over 100 degrees at some of the lower campgrounds, but those at the higher elevations and near the coast are mild. During the winter some of the higher campgrounds get snow, but the ones that were so hot during the summer offer great camping in mild temperatures.

Fire is a real and constant danger in large areas of the forest, and many campgrounds are closed during high fire danger times between July and November. At times the fire danger is so high no visitors, either day use or overnight, are allowed into large portions of the forest.

With over seventy campgrounds to choose from, and with such varying weather conditions, it is difficult to recommend special campgrounds in Los Padres. The best bet is to contact the rangers in the district you wish to visit to make sure that the campgrounds there are open and that the weather conditions are conducive to camping.

Hiking Activities

The over 1,500 miles of hiking trails in this large national forest offer numerous opportunities for hiking and backpacking. Many of these trails lead from the more than seventy campgrounds, and hiking is good to excellent near most camping sites.

The primary forest type in the region is chaparral cover, a thick, sharp scrub that is a combination of manzanita, ceonotheus, and buck brush that thrives on the hot, exposed slopes. At higher elevations stands of ponderosa pine offer shade and an open understory where hikers can explore easily.

The wilderness areas in the forest are located in some of the most rugged country along the coast. That makes hiking into the backcountry a strenuous chore that only the most motivated youngsters are willing to attempt.

Special Outings and Activities

As with most other national forests, special outings here are generally what you make them. Fishing is an extremely popular activity throughout the region, and swimming in larger streams is also popular.

The higher reaches of the national forest, primarily around Mt. Pinos, offer some winter sports, and a few campgrounds are open nearby for winter camping.

Some of the larger campgrounds have ranger programs and campfire talks, but most are small enough that rangers only check in during the day to make sure everything is okay.

MORRO BAY AREA STATE PARKS
c/o Morro Bay State Park
Morro Bay, CA 93442
(805) 772-2560

One state beach and two state parks are located along the ocean around Morro Bay. These offer campers a variety of choices ranging from campsites along the beach to ones in rugged canyons where the hillsides are dotted with coastal live oak.

At Morro Bay State Park one of the largest natural marsh-lands remaining along the California coast is home to count-less birds. Morro Strand State Beach offers good beachcombing, and Montana de Oro State Park has over fifty miles of trails that lead through canyons with year-round streams and along ridges where you can see the ocean to the west.

Recommended Ages
Excellent for all ages.

Location
The three parks are located to the west of State Route 1 around Morro Bay.

Camping Facilities
For developed campsites, head for Morro Bay State Park and Morro Strand State Beach. The state park has 115 developed sites that accommodate thirty-one-foot trailers and motor homes. It also has hot showers scattered throughout the camp-ground. The state beach has 104 developed sites that accom-modate twenty-four-foot trailers and motor homes and outdoor cold showers.

Montana de Oro State Park has fifty primitive sites along Islay Creek that accommodate twenty-four-foot trailers and motor homes, but have no showers.

Of the three campgrounds, Morro Bay State Park is the most developed and most crowded. Morro Strand is a beach campground with the sites strung along almost two miles of beach frontage. For camping with more of a feeling of wilder-ness, Montana de Oro is where you should head.

Morro Bay State Park is open and on the State Park Reser-vation System all year. Morro Strand and Montana de Oro are open year-round and on the State Park Reservation Sys-tem from mid-May through August.

Hiking Activities
Morro Strand offers great beach hiking along a 1.7-mile-long

beach, but for the best hiking head for Montana de Oro. This "Mountain of Gold" has over fifty miles of marked trails that lead to the top of nearby peaks, across the top of rugged cliffs, to secluded beaches, and through wooded canyons. The "gold" in its name comes from the colorful wildflowers that blanket the hillsides during the spring bloom, a great time to hike through the park.

There are two year-round streams that flow through the park and children like to hike the trails that follow these waterways. There is always plenty to do and see along the banks, and the youngest to the oldest can enjoy a short or long trek along these trails.

A short nature trail near the park office introduces you to the plants and animals that are native to the region, and even preschoolers can learn a lot about the region by following the self-guided path with their parents.

Special Outings and Activities

Swimming in the warm waters and lazing in the sun on the wide sand beaches are a special treat for those who come to

Many tidepools can be explored at low tide along the central coast.

this series of parks, but there are plenty of other activities available.

Fishing is good along the shore and in the streams that flow through Montana de Oro, and beachcombing for small shells and driftwood is great along Morro Strand.

In Morro Bay State Park, Los Osos Creek provides water for a large marsh as it opens out into Morro Bay. There, bird watching is great, for the marsh is one of the largest natural marshes left along the California coast.

Montana de Oro is not only great for hiking, but many of its trails have also been designated for horseback riding. There is even an equestrian camping area with corrals and water troughs for horses.

PFEIFFER–BIG SUR STATE PARK
Big Sur, CA 93920
(408) 667-2315

This 821-acre park is a great place to camp as you explore the Big Sur region. Although the park does not offer access to the ocean you can reach the coast easily along Sycamore Canyon Road to the south. There are only six miles of hiking trails within the park, but the adjoining Ventana Wilderness in the Los Padres National Forest has more than 200 miles of scenic trails.

This is one of the best, and most popular, family camping sites in California and is busy all year.

Recommended Ages
Excellent for all ages.

Location
The park is twenty-six miles south of Carmel on State Route 1.

Camping Facilities
This is a full-service campground with 217 sites scattered throughout the park in four areas. All are near the banks of the Big Sur River. The sites are shaded, accommodate twenty-

Windswept marine terraces are great places to hike near parks along the central coast.

seven-foot trailers and thirty-two-foot motor homes, and have showers located in restrooms throughout the sites.

There are even some concession-operated motel-like cabins for rent in the park for those who want to have the experience of camping but don't want to sleep on the ground.

The campground is open and on the State Park Reservation System year-round.

Hiking Activities

With trails that range from less than half a mile to four miles in length even young children can join in the fun of hiking along the river, through redwood groves, to year-round waterfalls, and to the top of peaks with great views of the ocean to the west.

The shortest trail is a self-guided nature trail near the park headquarters and campfire center, and the longest that is completely within the park is the Buzzards Roost Trail on the west side of State Route 1.

My favorite trail leads up into the Big Sur Gorge to the east of the park. This trail leads into wilderness quickly, and children like to scramble over boulders along the Big Sur River as they head upstream.

For those who want a little longer hike, and who want to do an overnight or two, a number of trails lead into the Ventana Wilderness of the Los Padres National Forest. There, over 200 miles of trails lead through some of the wildest and most rugged country on the central coast.

Special Outings and Activities

Children use the Big Sur River for swimming and fishing, and a short drive takes you to the coast where you can hike along the top of steep cliffs as you watch for nesting sea birds, migrating whales, and sea otters frolicking in the surf just offshore.

There is an active Junior Ranger program during the day, and rangers also lead hikes for adults, children, and families. At night they hold campfire talks that introduce campers to the natural history of the Big Sur region.

PINNACLES NATIONAL MONUMENT
Paicines, CA 95043
(408) 389-4578

Caves, rock spires, and tall pinnacles created by erosion of ancient volcanic activity stand above rugged chaparral country in this 16,221-acre park. These formations tower from 1,200 to 3,300 feet above the rolling hills that surround them.

Summer temperatures rise above 100 degrees regularly, while midwinter is generally wet. This makes spring and fall the favorite times to visit the park. In spring vibrant wildflowers cover the slopes and bird life is abundant among the chaparral.

Recommended Ages
Poor to Good for toddlers and preschoolers, Excellent for 6–9 and for 10 and over.

Location

The west entrance to the Chaparral Ranger Station and Campground is twelve miles south of Soledad on State Route 146.

Camping Facilities

Camping is limited in this park, and on the east side of the park there is a private campground just before you enter the park. On the west is the Chaparral Campground with twenty-four walk-in sites. No trailers or motor homes are accommodated.

Although over twenty-five miles of developed trails lead into the backcountry, no backcountry camping is allowed within the monument.

No reservations are accepted for the campground, which is open year-round.

Hiking Activities

Hiking is the centerpiece of this wild land atop the San Andreas Fault. Chaparral covers the steep slopes where summer temperatures frequently top 100 degrees and caves dot the hillsides.

Short nature trails near the Chaparral Ranger Station on the west side of the monument and the Bear Gulch Visitor Center on the east side offer you a great introduction to the natural history of the region and prepare you for longer hikes into the backcountry.

More short trails are available near Bear Gulch, but no roads connect the Chaparral Campground with the east side. To reach it you must either make a day's drive or hike over the ridge. Neither is appropriate for families with young children, so I recommend that you stick to the hikes near the ranger station.

Special Outings and Activities

Two activities are special here, and neither is particularly appropriate for younger children. The first is technical rock climbing. For families with a good background in technical climbing, this is a great place to take younger climbers to learn the ropes.

The other activity, which younger children can participate in if they don't mind being in dark places, is caving. Caves were formed in the region by the violent actions of the San Andreas Fault, and rangers can direct you to the caves most appropriate for your family's abilities and desires.

Most of the caves have very low ceilings and slippery floors, so have a good flashlight for every member of your party, and make sure everyone is wearing shoes appropriate for the slippery surfaces.

PORTOLA STATE PARK
Star Route 2
La Honda, CA 94020
(415) 948-9098

Two year-round streams cut through almost 10,000 acres of redwoods, Douglas fir, and coast live oak in the state and county parks that join together in this rugged basin.

Developed campsites, walk-in trail camps, and group camps all offer great access to hiking trails in the parks.

Recommended Ages
Poor to Good for toddlers and preschoolers, Excellent for 6–9 and for 10 and over.

Location
The park is in southern San Mateo County, seven miles southwest of Skyline Boulevard on Alpine Road.

Camping Facilities
The campground has fifty-two sites that accommodate twenty-four-foot trailers and twenty-seven-foot motor homes. Showers are scattered throughout the campground.

The campground is open and on the State Park Reservation System year-round.

Hiking Activities

The fifteen miles of hiking trails within the park connect with miles of other trails that lead into the adjoining county and regional parks. All lead through great stands of redwoods that tower over 250 feet above the slopes. The trails are steep in spots, and only those near the campground are easy for preschoolers and toddlers. Children do enjoy the self-guided nature trail near the park headquarters, however.

This is a good park to bring children ten and over because you can take long, strenuous hikes that tire them out, thereby ensuring a good night's sleep for everyone.

Special Outings and Activities

Younger children, and even teens, like to try their luck fishing in the two year-round streams that flow through the park. Although they are not likely to make any major catches, they may haul in a bullhead, crawdad, or small trout.

Children can participate in the Junior Ranger program during the day. Rangers lead hikes for adults, children, and families. At night you can join with other campers at the campfire circle where rangers lead talks about the local ecology. There are also nature exhibits at the headquarters where the whole family can learn about the local natural history.

CHAPTER 4

CENTRAL INLAND CAMPING

Most families who camp in this region head for the central and southern Sierra. There, meadows blanketed with spring wildflowers, streams fed by snowmelt waters, and deep, blue lakes attract campers who want to stretch their legs and expand their lungs. Scenic trails lead out of almost all campgrounds into the high country of the Sierra, where glacier-carved granite rises above tree level and lakes become sapphires in low-lying cirque basins—basins where glaciers met their end thousands of years ago.

The western slopes of the Sierra are covered with thick conifer forests of pine, fir, and incense cedar. These thrive on the moisture-rich slopes fed by heavy winter storms that move in from the Pacific and drop dozens of feet of snow each winter.

This heavy snow precludes winter camping in most of the region, but thousands of families head for the higher elevations to enjoy winter sports even if they can't camp under clear skies.

When the higher campgrounds are closed for the winter, a number in the Gold Rush country that extends along the western foothills of the Sierra are open and provide excellent winter camping during the lull between storms.

Central Inland Camping

KEY TO PARKS

1. *Caswell Memorial State Park*
2. *Calaveras Big Trees State Park*
3. *Death Valley National Park*
4. *Grover Hot Springs State Park*
5. *Henry W. Coe State Park*
6. *Indian Grinding Rock State Historic Park*
7. *Inyo National Forest*
8. *Kings Canyon National Park*
9. *Mount Diabolo State Park*
10. *Sequoia National Forest*
11. *Sequoia National Park*
12. *Sierra National Forest*
13. *Stanislaus National Forest*
14. *Toiyabe National Forest*
15. *Yosemite National Park*

Several campgrounds in the Central Valley preserve remnants of the vast wetlands and oak riparian forests and also offer excellent winter camping. These sites are often located in good birding locations where you can see bald eagles, sandhill cranes, numerous waterfowl, and migrating songbirds during the spring and fall.

The eastern slopes of the Sierra are drier, but the highest elevations still receive heavy snowpacks each winter. Death Valley is the premier winter destination for family camping on the east side of the Sierra, and the higher slopes offer some of the state's best wildflower displays in early summer.

The hiking along the eastern slope of the high Sierra is unsurpassed. Trails lead along exposed granite ridges above deep canyons, and blue cirque lakes dot the landscape below.

The central inland region is second only to the north inland region for diversity of camping sites and is a popular destination for families from Southern California who wish to escape the torrid heat of the deserts during midsummer.

CASWELL MEMORIAL STATE PARK
28000 South Austin Road
Ripon, CA 95366
(209) 599-3810

Once large groves of valley live oak dominated the landscape of riverbanks and floodplains across the Central Valley, but today only small remnants of these majestic forests still stand. One of them is in this park along the Stanislaus River.

Hiking trails lead through groves of oak more than sixty feet tall with girths exceeding seventeen feet. These trails lead to protected beaches where children can swim or fish.

Recommended Ages
Excellent for all ages.

Location
The park is on Austin Road, six miles south of Ripon and State Route 99.

Camping Facilities
The sixty-five-site campground lies within a sweeping curve of the Stanislaus River as it winds its way across the San Joaquin Valley to the Sacramento/San Joaquin Delta. The developed sites have showers placed among the campground, and tall oak provide shade against the summer sun of the hot valley. The sites accommodate twenty-one-foot trailers and twenty-four-foot motor homes.

The campground is open year-round and on the State Park Reservation System from May through September.

Hiking Activities
This park is great for hiking with preschoolers and toddlers. The level trails wind through dense groves of valley oak, willow, and cottonwood. Other trails lead to the meandering path of the river and follow along its banks.

None of the hikes challenge physically fit older children, yet kids love to explore among the undergrowth of this remnant of the hardwood riparian forest that once covered much of the flood plains of the Central Valley.

Bird watching is great in the forest, and a blue heron rookery is located along the river near the park boundary. From March to May you can view the antics of mating heron and the frantic feeding activities after the young birds hatch.

Special Outings and Activities
Fishing is good to excellent in the river all year, and even adults enjoy spending a leisurely afternoon with a fishing line submerged in the murky waters. Striped and black bass are always plentiful, as well as pan fish such as crappie, blue gill, and perch. Catfish are also abundant. In the fall there is even some salmon fishing along the river as they migrate upstream to their spawning grounds.

Young children like to watch this migration even if they aren't interested in fishing. The salmon are frequently active during the day, and you can see them as they move from pool to pool through shallow ripples.

Willow and oak rise from the shallows of waterways to form thick riparian forests rich with wildlife in such parks as Caswell Memorial State Park in the Central Valley.

During the warm summers children flock to the swimming hole and beach near the day-use area. The river here gently slopes from the beach into deeper water. Toddlers enjoy playing along the edge. Older children like to hunt among the forest understory for signs of animals such as raccoon, fox, coyote, and opossum. These are all abundant because they feed off water creatures and small birds that flourish near the river.

Natural history exhibits at the park office give a good introduction to the animals that live in the area and where to locate them. Rangers lead occasional hikes and present talks at evening campfires during the summer.

The last Sunday in February the park hosts the Great Valley Tule Fog Fete, which features a pea soup cook-off and plenty of activities for children.

CALAVERAS BIG TREES STATE PARK
P.O. Box 120
Arnold, CA 95223
(209) 795-2334

Trails lead from two campgrounds into large stands of giant sequoia. There you can hike among the largest of all living things. These giants are members of a species that has grown in the region since the Mesozoic Age when dinosaurs still roamed the earth.

The park straddles both the Stanislaus River and Beaver Creek, where visitors can fish or swim during the warm summers. Since the park stays open all year, more and more people head for it during midwinter to camp near snowshoe and cross-country ski opportunities.

Recommended Ages
Excellent for all ages.

Location
The park is four miles northeast of Arnold on State Route 4.

Camping Facilities
Two campgrounds (North Grove and Oak Hollow) have 129 developed sites that accommodate twenty-seven-foot trailers and motor homes. Showers are found throughout both campgrounds. North Grove is the most developed and busiest of the two; the sites at Oak Hollow, which I prefer, are more secluded. There are also several environmental campsites for those who want to backpack in a short distance. The campfire center, visitor center, and natural history exhibits are all near the North Grove Campground.

The campgrounds are open year-round and on the State Park Reservation System from May through September.

Hiking Activities
For younger children, and as an introduction to the ecology of the area for everyone, take the self-guided nature trails that

wind through both the large groves of big trees in the park. Both these short trails are good for advanced toddlers and preschoolers, and older children who have never seen giant sequoia will be enthralled by their magnificence as they walk by such examples as the Big Stump. A dance hall was once built here, using the flat surface of the stump as the dance floor.

Longer hikes lead farther into the forests and along Beaver Creek and the Stanislaus River.

Special Outings and Activities
During the warmer months of summer children gravitate to the cool waters of Beaver Creek and the Stanislaus River where they enjoy diving into the deeper pools off large boulders. Younger children find shallow pools where they can wade and soak to cool off. The same waterways provide adequate fishing for those who are more interested in sedentary activities.

There are nature exhibits at the visitor center and ranger-led hikes and campfire talks.

DEATH VALLEY NATIONAL MONUMENT
Superintendent
Death Valley, CA 92328
(619) 786-2331

Badwater, Scotty's Castle, Zabriske Point, Furnace Creek, Ubehabe Crater, Artists Drive. These are just a few of the sites in Death Valley, newly designated as a national park. High mountains with steep canyons surround the low flatlands of the valley—the lowest point in the U.S.

In the spring wildflowers are spectacular along the valley floor, and hikes among the sand dunes warm cold bones. There is more to do in the park than just explore the sights in the valley: In the high mountains you can camp near braying wild burros and climb to the top of 10,000-foot peaks. There is even a waterfall in the middle of the desert for those who want to explore an out-of-the-way canyon.

One fact that is obvious to first-time visitors is that Death Valley is extremely large. The distances between sites is so great that it is almost impossible to make an easy day trip. Going from one site to another takes a whole day and puts the family in the car for hours on end.

I like to explore the region by camping at a different campground every couple of days, making shorter trips out from the campgrounds to nearby sites.

Recommended Ages
Poor for toddlers and preschoolers (some older preschoolers may enjoy it), Excellent for 6–9 and for 10 and over.

Location
The park lies between U.S. 95 to the east in Nevada and U.S. 395 to the west in California.

Camping Facilities
There are seven campgrounds for tents and RVs with 1,548 sites, and three backcountry campgrounds for hike-in and four-wheel-drive vehicles with twenty sites for tents. Of these, three campgrounds are at or near sea level in the valley itself. Only Furnace Creek, with 156 sites is open year-round, while Sunset, with 1,000 sites, and Stove Pipe Wells, with 200 sites, are open from November through April. Emigrant Campground, with only 10 sites, lies at 2,100 feet and is open April through October.

Higher up is Wildrose at 4,100 feet. This thirty-six-site campground is open all year but does not have water. This does not make it totally undesirable, though, for it is much cooler than in the valley below, and feral donkeys enliven the nights with their braying on the hillsides above.

Thorndike and Mahogany Flat, at 7,500 and 8,200 feet respectively, are open only from March through November because of winter snows. These are great places to camp in the summer, however, for few people head for these out-of-the-way places in the park. They are too far away from the main attractions of the valley for day trips, though, so you should head there when you plan on enjoying the hikes to nearby peaks and lazing about with no worries or timetable. You must provide your own water for these sites also.

Hiking Activities
Death Valley isn't thought of as a hiking park, but during the cooler months children enjoy hiking over the sand dunes, across the weathered ridges of Dante's View and Zabriske Point, around Ubehabe Crater, and among other attractions.

In the summer there are great hikes to peaks near Wildrose and Mahogany Flat. At the latter you can head for the top of Telescope Peak. From there you'll see the lowest point in the continental U.S., near Badwater to the east, and the highest point at Mt. Whitney, to the west, by simply turning around.

Special Outings and Activities
The whole of Death Valley is a special outing. No other place in the country has so much lore of desert tribulations and sites such as Scotty's Castle, Hell's Gate, and the Borax Museum, where you can discover more about the trials of early settlers in the region.

Since the park is so large, and the sites are so varied, I suggest that you thoroughly investigate what is available in the park long before you head there. Then you can choose which campgrounds you want to stay in and for how long before you head out on your trip.

In early November the park hosts the Death Valley Fall Festival and Death Valley 49ers Encampment, two events that are exciting, entertaining, and educational. More than 40,000 people convene for the 49ers Encampment so you may not want to try to get a camping spot during it, but the fall festival is smaller and more focused on activities for kids.

GROVER HOT SPRINGS STATE PARK
P.O. Box 188
Markleeville, CA 96120
(916) 694-2248

The favorite activity in this park is soaking in the hot pools fed by six underground mineral springs. The springs keep the pools between 102 and 105 degrees. The runoff from the pools feeds into nearby Hot Springs Creek, which flows through the large meadow in the middle of the park throughout the year. Even the cold of the high country does not freeze the creek as the meadow fills with snow.

The pools are open all year, although the campground closes in early October each fall.

Recommended Ages
Good for toddlers and preschoolers, Excellent for 6–9 and for 10 and over.

Location
The park is three miles west of Markleeville on Hot Springs Road.

Camping Facilities
Two campgrounds here have seventy-six developed sites. Each has showers located in restrooms throughout the campground, and the sites accommodate twenty-four-foot trailers and twenty-seven-foot motor homes. Both campgrounds are located along Hot Springs Creek in the middle of a large meadow.

The campground is open and on the State Park Reservation System from May through September. Although the campground is not open in the winter, camping is allowed in the picnic area near the park entrance for those who come to enjoy the hot springs and cross-country skiing during the winter.

Hiking Activities
The Transition Walk Nature Trail leads along Hot Springs Creek, across a meadow, and along an old irrigation ditch before returning to the trailhead near the Quaking Aspen Campground. This is a great short hike for even advanced toddlers, and the rest of the family can learn about the natural history of the region as they hike it.

The eastern side of the Sierra offers hot springs where you can enjoy warm soaks even when snow is visible in the distance.

Longer trails lead to Burnside Lake and along Sawmill Creek. These lead into the high country above the hot springs where alpine meadows offer spectacular flower blooms in early and late summer.

Special Outings and Activities

Soaking in the pool fed by the hot springs is by far the most special activity here, but other activities include an active Junior Ranger program, ranger-led day hikes, and campfire talks most nights. Rangers also lead visitors to other hot springs in the region, such as Carson River Hot Springs, during the summer, and offer cross-country skiing and snowshoeing lessons in the winter.

Hot Springs Creek and nearby feeder streams offer good trout fishing all summer, and even young fishermen frequently catch a batch of planted trout for dinner.

The valleys around the Carson River are among the best color spots in California during the fall.

HENRY W. COE STATE PARK
P.O. Box 846
Morgan Hill, CA 95038
(408) 779-2728

This 68,000-acre park is primarily undeveloped, with only primitive campsites for car campers and hike-in campsites for backpackers. Those who like solitude and wilderness head here. The most popular seasons are spring and fall when the weather is dry and temperate. During midsummer the temperatures rise above 100 degrees regularly, and winters are wet and cold.

This park has 125 miles of trails that lead through the rugged slopes of the Hamilton Range.

Recommended Ages
Poor for toddlers, Good for older preschoolers, Excellent for 6–9 and for 10 and over.

Location
The park is fourteen miles east of Morgan Hill on East Dunne Avenue.

Camping Facilities
The primitive campsites here accommodate eighteen-foot trailers and twenty-six-foot motor homes. Individual sites do not have water, but there is water available at park headquarters. There are also twenty-one sites for backpackers spread throughout the park.

Although the campground and backcountry sites are open all year, fire danger during the hot, dry days of midsummer and early fall may force the closure of the park for either overnight or day use.

There are three equestrian camping sites with corrals, water, and hitching rails at headquarters, at Manzanita Point, and at Shaffer's Corral. These accommodate from eight to thirty riders and horses.

Hiking Activities

There is little hiking here for younger children, but for those ten and over there is almost unlimited hiking over more than forty miles of trails that lead across open grassland into oak forests, and to the top of ridges that overlook the Santa Clara Valley to the west. Children six to nine years old enjoy the hikes to Frog Lake and Madrone Soda Springs.

As I mentioned earlier, most people visit this park in the spring and fall when the weather is moderate and the rains have either ceased or not yet begun. During the spring the hills are covered with bright carpets of wildflowers that add a vibrant contrast to the emerald of the new year's grasses.

Special Outings and Activities

Swimming in the various streams that crisscross the park is a favorite activity here before they dry up late in the summer. There is also fishing in these streams, as well as in the several reservoirs that dot the old ranch land.

The Pine Ridge Museum at park headquarters interprets ranch life of the 1880s in the region, and children like to explore for various historic sites after they visit the museum.

INDIAN GRINDING ROCK STATE HISTORIC PARK
14881 Pine Grove-Volcano Road
Pine Grove, CA 95665
(209) 296-7488

This historic park is a favorite of children of all ages who like to explore the history of the Native Americans living in the region long before European explorers arrived on the scene. Reconstructed dwellings, a roundhouse, and an Indian football field are all near a developed campground. Several trails lead through the 136-acre park.

Recommended Ages

Poor for toddlers, Good for preschoolers, Excellent for 6–9 and for 10 and over.

Location

The park is twelve miles northeast of Jackson on Pine Grove-Volcano Road.

Camping Facilities

There are twenty-one developed sites in this small campground. There are no showers, but the sites do accommodate twenty-seven-foot trailers and motor homes.

The campground is open and on the State Park Reservation System year-round.

Hiking Activities

A short nature trail leads through a wooded area near the reconstructed Indian village, and a longer trail leads around the small park. These two trails are good even for advanced toddlers, and all ages enjoy exploring the village, a roundhouse, and a mortar rock where Native Americans ground acorns into meal for hundreds—if not thousands—of years.

There are no long hikes in the park so you can let your older children explore on their own along the trails.

Special Outings and Activities

The museum here is one of the most complete Native American museums in any state park in California, and children love to study the exhibits before exploring the village and grinding rock. Rangers lead hikes through the reconstructed village during the day and give campfire talks at night during the busy season.

The seasonal creek is a favorite spot for young children when it is running, but watch for rattlesnakes when it is dry.

INYO NATIONAL FOREST

Forest Supervisor
873 North Main Street
Bishop, CA 93514
(619) 873-2400

The southernmost glacier in the U.S. is located within this

2-million-acre national forest. Other features include a 4,600-year-old bristlecone pine; the largest Jeffrey pine forest in the world; and Mt. Whitney, the highest peak in the contiguous U.S.

The forest is a popular destination for both winter and summer sports, and has nearly 500 lakes and more than 100 streams where the fishing is excellent.

There are five wilderness areas and four ranger districts. Both the Pacific Crest and John Muir Trails traverse the region, and other hiking trails lead into some of the most photographed sites in the Sierra Nevada.

Recommended Ages
Good to Excellent for all ages.

Location
The forest covers about 160 square miles of the eastern Sierra Nevada to the east of Yosemite and Sequoia National Parks. U.S. 395 runs between the two sections of the forest that extend from Mono Lake in the north to State Route 178 in the south.

Camping Facilities
All I can say about camping in this national forest is that you can't go wrong. With over seventy choice campgrounds in four of the most scenic national forest ranger districts in the country there is an incredible selection of camping sites that will satisfy even the most discriminating campers.

For seclusion and privacy I head for the many intimate campgrounds in the White Mountain Ranger District. These include campgrounds high in an ancient bristlecone pine forest to the east of Big Pine in the White Mountains, as well as alpine campgrounds along Bishop and Rock creeks high in the eastern Sierra Nevada.

For more developed campgrounds near a popular resort area try the campgrounds in the Mammoth Lakes Basin and Reds Meadow Drainage near Mammoth Lakes Village and

Campers from several forest service and county campgrounds can head for the shores of Mono Lake to walk among the tufa formations.

Devils Postpile National Monument. While these are more crowded, and many require advance reservations, they do give families a chance to get out into the wilderness without being too far from civilization.

The campgrounds in the Mono Lake Ranger District are somewhat in between White Mountain Ranger District and Mammoth Lakes Basin. Some campgrounds are large, close to town, and heavily used. Others are more off the beaten path, high in the eastern Sierra, and lightly used.

Choose what you want in a campground and then call the ranger district of your choice to ask about site availability. If the large, well-developed campgrounds are full you may still be able to find a site in one of the smaller, nearby campgrounds.

Hiking Activities

If hiking in an alpine setting is what you like, this is the place to go. From the John Muir Trail to dozens of smaller forest service trails there is a hike for almost everyone. Trails lead out from every campground into higher country where meadows are awash in alpine flower blossoms in early summer and deep blue lakes fill the bottom of glacier cirques formed as the glaciers retreated in the last ice age.

You may even encounter a small glacier on these hikes and get a chance to hike across it during late summer when the daytime temperatures allow you to hike in shorts and tank tops. Of course, at this elevation you must be very careful to avoid sunburns. Keep your sunscreen on all the time.

While many of the hikes are too strenuous for younger kids, some near the campgrounds are perfect for introducing preschoolers to the joy of high country hiking. They love to

High-altitude hikes often lead to snow fields even in late summer.

explore along the banks of mountain streams, whose ice-cold water turns extremities blue with only the slightest dousing, and to climb to low ridges where they can enjoy views over alpine valleys and meadows.

Special Outings and Activities
As with all national forest campgrounds you make your own special outings and activities. Some of the larger, more developed campgrounds do have resident rangers who lead walks during the day and give campfire talks at night, but the majority of the campgrounds in this national forest are too small to support such activities. That is fine with me, and with many families who like to take their own hikes and watch the stars in the crystal clear skies at night.

KINGS CANYON NATIONAL PARK
Superintendent
Sequoia and Kings Canyon National Parks
Three Rivers, CA 93271
(209) 565-3456

General Grant Grove is the top attraction in this 461,636-acre national park, but the grove makes up only a very small part of the park. More than 800 miles of trails lead to over 1,000 glacial lakes nestled in pockets of granite, many at above 10,000 feet elevation.

The John Muir Trail wanders through the eastern portion of the park's backcountry on its way south to Mt. Whitney.

Recommended Ages
Poor for toddlers, Good for preschoolers, and Excellent for 6–9 and for 10 and over.

Location
Take State Route 180 east from Fresno to the park.

Camping Facilities
Seven campgrounds with over 725 sites are located near two

of the park's groves: Grant and Cedar. Near Grant Grove are Azalea, Crystal Springs, and Sunset campgrounds. Of these only Azalea is open year-round. The others are open from late April to November.

Near Cedar Grove are Moraine, Canyon View, Sheep Creek, and Sentinel campgrounds. These are open approximately from late April to November, although they may open as late as Memorial Day after winters of heavy snowfall.

No reservations are accepted at any of the campgrounds, and you should try to arrive late on a Sunday afternoon or early on a Monday morning to find a vacant site during midsummer.

Hiking Activities

Hiking is exceptional in this large park, both for young children who can only make short, level hikes and for older ones who like to stretch their legs on long, strenuous hikes.

There are self-guided nature trails at both groves that lead you past the largest of these gigantic trees. Longer hikes take you into the backcountry to the Valley of the Kings, which John Muir thought to be even grander than Yosemite. This canyon is one of the deepest gorges in North America and offers outstanding vistas along its many trails.

A good trail for slightly older youth is the river trail that leads out of Cedar Grove to Roaring River Falls and Zumwalt Meadow. This is a good day hike and you can take a long lunch break at the meadow.

Special Outings and Activities

While visiting big trees and viewing one of the deepest gorges in America are special in themselves, there are plenty of other special things to do at this national park.

Bicycles can be rented at Cedar Grove or you can bring your own to bicycle along winding roads and lightly used dirt roads (check with the rangers before taking a bicycle on any park trail because they are prohibited on most), or you can take horseback rides from stables at both Cedar and Grant groves.

Fishing is good in the lakes and streams of the park, and there are several waterfalls you can hike to in the backcountry. There the older kids like to swim in the cold waters beneath the falls.

There is a large visitor center at Grant Grove, and a complete offering of ranger-led nature walks during the summer months. During the summer the nature center becomes a hands-on science museum where kids can feel and touch items as they learn about the natural history of the region. Rangers also lead campfire talks at both Grant and Cedar Grove campgrounds.

The park has a free newspaper, *The Sequoia Bark*, that provides current information about family activities in the park. You can get one at the park entrance or visitor center, or by calling the park before your visit and having one mailed to you.

MOUNT DIABLO STATE PARK
P.O. Box 250
Diablo, CA 94528
(510) 837-2525

The view from the top of Mt. Diablo is said to be second only to Mt. Kilimanjaro as to the number of square miles seen. On clear days, which unfortunately don't come as frequently as they once did, you can see almost 200 miles, with views of Mt. Shasta to the north and Yosemite to the east and south. The park also has some of the best wildflower displays found in northern California.

Recommended Ages
Good to excellent for all ages.

Location
The park is five miles east of Danville and I-680 on Diablo Road.

Camping Facilities
Three campgrounds provide sixty developed sites, which

seems like a small number considering how close the park is to a major population center. Most of the visitors to the park are there for day use, however, and there are almost always vacant sites.

Juniper Campground is the only one that accommodates trailers and motor homes. It accepts nineteen-foot trailers and thirty-one-foot motor homes. There are no showers at any of the campgrounds.

The area is one of high fire danger and the campgrounds are available on a first-come, first-served basis during the summer months primarily due to the possibility of last-minute park closures because of extreme fire danger. The campgrounds are on the State Park Reservation System between October and May, but you are likely to find a site even if you have not reserved one.

There is equestrian camping at Barbecue Terrace and Pioneer Camp. There is space for eighty-four horses and riders with stalls and water trough at Barbecue Terrace, and you can trailer to the site. Pioneer Camp is much smaller, with space for eight horses and riders. There are stalls and water troughs, and you can trailer to this site also.

Six environmental campsites are located in Curry Canyon and Black Hills areas. They are about a mile from the parking area, and you can use them only after the fire season has passed. This is generally between October 1 and May 31.

Hiking Activities
Hiking is excellent in the park except during the summer when temperatures often exceed 100 degrees. Trails lead out of all three campgrounds, and even preschoolers enjoy hiking along the trails when the grasses are green and the wildflowers are adding bursts of vibrant colors to the emerald green of the slopes.

The longer trails are for the well-conditioned, however, because the slopes here are steep and the distance between trailheads is generally several miles.

Special Outings and Activities
Wildflower watching is the really special activity in the park and this usually peaks between late February and early May. During that period you can't beat this park for its beautiful wildflowers. Rangers lead wildflower walks to some of the more spectacular blooms. They also give occasional campfire talks at night.

SEQUOIA NATIONAL FOREST
Forest Supervisor
900 West Grand Avenue
Porterville, CA 93257
(209) 784-1500

This national forest includes over a million acres of the Sierra Nevada, and contains thirty groves of giant Sequoia. While this magnificent tree is a major attraction, there are plenty of other recreational activities available within the region.

Spectacular waterfalls, frigid mountain streams, miles of trails that lead into the high country, and white-water rafting on the Kern River all add to the lure of this forest.

The forest has five wilderness areas and five ranger districts. There are forty-eight campgrounds scattered around the region.

Recommended Ages
Poor to Good for toddlers and preschoolers, Excellent for 6–9 and for 10 and over.

Location
This national forest covers the southern end of the Sierra Nevada and reaches from the Kings River in the north to the Kern River in the south. It extends west to east from the Sierra foothills along the San Joaquin Valley to the crest of the Sierra.

Camping Facilities
Unlike many national forests in the Sierra Nevada, Sequoia

National Forest offers campgrounds at a variety of elevations that make camping in it possible year-round. There are campgrounds at just about every 1,000 feet change in elevation, with the lowest found at 1,000 feet, and the highest at almost 8,000 feet. This gives families a great choice in what type of weather and temperature they want to enjoy on a camping outing.

The Hume Lake Ranger District, located to the east of Fresno, has the most campgrounds of any ranger district in the national forest, and several of these are large, well developed, and extremely popular. Princess Campground near Hume Lake offers ninety sites with all the amenities: showers, sites for trailers and motor homes, laundry facilities, and a nearby store. At 5,900 feet, days there may get a little warm, but the nights cool down to a level pleasant for sleeping. Nearby is the seventy-five-site Hume Lake Campground with the same services.

On the other end of the spectrum are Big Meadow and Buck Rock campgrounds with twenty-five and five sites, respectively. These two are located in a secluded section of the forest and offer no services, not even piped water. What they do offer is an opportunity to enjoy the backcountry of the High Sierra (they are at 7,600 feet) with few people around to bother you. The scenery is great, the hiking is excellent, the night skies are wonderful, and they are at the end of the road. What else could you ask for?

The next most popular ranger district in the forest is Cannell Meadows. All the campgrounds in this district have over twenty sites and water, and all accommodate trailers and motor homes up to twenty-seven feet. A number of them sit beside State Route 99 as it heads north from Lake Isabella along the Kern River. The lower campgrounds are at 3,000 and 4,000 feet, and daytime temperatures get high during midsummer, but campers can enjoy the fast flowing waters of the Kern before they reach the lake below.

Four great campgrounds lie at 7,000 to 8,000 feet around the edges of the South Sierra and Dome Land wilderness areas of the southern Sierra. These include Fish Creek and Troy, Kennedy, and Horse meadows. All of these are popular and well used, but they are located in one of the most scenic regions in the southern Sierra Nevada.

Hiking Activities

As always, there are an abundance of hiking trails that lead out from all of the forest service campgrounds. These take you into the backcountry where groves of giant sequoia stand high above slopes and where large granite outcroppings offer great vistas of deep gorges.

Some of the easy trails near the campgrounds are fine for toddlers and preschoolers, but I would not attempt to take any kids younger than nine on the longer and more difficult backcountry hikes.

A word of warning. This is bear country and you are very likely to encounter at least fresh signs of this large mammal as you hike along the trails. There is little to fear from these behemoths, however, as long as you pay attention and don't separate a mother from her cubs. At any other time the bear is likely to be more afraid of you than you are of it.

Special Outings and Activities

As with almost all national forest campgrounds you have to find your own special outings. Luckily, there are plenty in this national forest. From locating trees so huge that you can literally drive through them to chancing upon the ideal spot to photograph the wild backcountry, there are a wide variety of scenic outings to take near the campgrounds.

An extremely popular activity is white-water rafting on the Kern and King rivers that run through the national forest. With a gradient exceeding thirty feet per mile, the Kern is one of the steepest and wildest white-water rafting rivers in California. The King is less turbulent, and you can take younger kids on trips down it from above Mill Flat Campground in the Hume Lake District.

Swimming and fishing are also popular along the rivers

and streams of the forest, as well as in the lakes and reservoirs that are scattered throughout the region.

SEQUOIA NATIONAL PARK
Superintendent, Sequoia and Kings Canyon National Parks
Three Rivers, CA 93271
(209) 565-3456

More than 280,000 acres of this 402,487-acre national park are designated as wilderness. I am always surprised at how little development has been allowed within the rest of the park, especially since it is so close to heavily developed Yosemite National Park.

Deep canyons, great groves of giant Sequoia, and Mineral King Valley, a spectacular high alpine meadow that was once doomed to development as a ski resort by the Disney Corporation, are all popular destinations in the park. Seven campgrounds that range in elevation from 2,100 to 7,500 feet are spread throughout the park.

Recommended Ages
Poor for toddlers, Good for preschoolers, Excellent for 6–9 and for 10 and over.

Location
Take State Route 198 from State Route 99 to the southern entrance to the park.

Camping Facilities
There are two monstrous campgrounds, Dorst with 238 sites and Lodgepole with 260, near the park headquarters and the General Sherman tree, and three smaller ones not too far away.

The five have a total of 583 sites, and do fill up during midsummer. The smaller ones tend to fill last, and they are my preference anyway. They are not so close to the hustle and bustle of tour buses, day visitors, and general store customers. If you wish to make reservations, however, you have little choice. Lodgepole is the only campground in the park on a reservation system, and then only from Memorial Day through Labor Day, although it is open all year.

Farther away from the center of action in the park, and in a completely different ecosystem, are the two campgrounds at Mineral King. These are accessible only by about thirty miles of extremely curvy mountain roads, but they are well worth the effort. The alpine valley where Cold Springs Campground sits is one of the best in the Sierra that you can drive to.

The campgrounds at higher elevations in the park are only open from Memorial Day to Labor Day, but three of the ones near General Sherman are open all year, with an occasional closing due to heavy winter snows.

Hiking Activities
There is a hike in this park for everyone. From short self-guided nature trails near the major campgrounds to long, strenuous backcountry hikes above the tree line, you can't miss here.

Even toddlers and preschoolers enjoy the nature trails as they wind in and out of giant trees, many of which have fallen on their sides to form homes for the children's imaginary creatures.

From the campgrounds at Mineral King, trails lead into alpine backcountry where lakes abound. Hiking is strenuous as you wind up treeless slopes and over sharp ridges. Many shorter, less strenuous trails lead to sites such as the Squatter's Cabin, Tharp's Log, and Trail of the Sequoias in the main section of the park.

A good, short, but strenuous, hike that kids like is the climb to the top of Moro Rock. This granite monolith juts upward from the edge of the forest to provide a great vista of the Kaweah River Canyon below. You climb up steep granite steps for 300 vertical feet to the top of the 6,725-foot peak.

Special Outings and Activities
Before engaging in any special activity within the park you

should visit one of the visitor centers at Lodgepole or Ash Mountain, or the ranger station at Mineral King. There you can learn about all the many hikes, nature walks, and campfire talks that are a regular part of the park's offerings during the summer.

There are numerous ranger-led walks and hikes that the whole family can enjoy, a Junior Ranger program for older kids, and campfire talks every evening at Dorst, Potwisha, and Lodgepole campgrounds. There are no campfire programs at the two Mineral King campgrounds.

Horseback riding is available at the Wolverton Pack Station near Lodgepole and at Mineral King. Fishing in the streams and lakes of the backcountry is good for trout, and older kids like to make that part of a day's outing.

A very special outing is a visit to Crystal Cave. This is a marble cave with formations left from water dripping for millennia through cracks in the rock above. Although not quite as large as the better known Oregon Caves National Monument, Crystal Cave is every bit as captivating and makes a great afternoon outing when everyone is just a bit bored.

SIERRA NATIONAL FOREST
Forest Supervisor
1600 Tollhouse Road
Clovis, CA 93611-0532
(209) 487-5155

Only one major road enters this national forest high in the Sierra Nevada. With elevations between 900 and 13,986 feet, the extremes in the forest are great. From the low chaparral of the lower elevations, through dense forest in the middle, to granite peaks above tree level you can pick and choose the type of area where you wish to camp.

There are four ranger districts with over sixty campgrounds and five wilderness areas in the 1.4 million acres of the forest.

Recommended Ages
Good to Excellent for all ages.

Location
To the north of the forest boundaries lies Yosemite National Park. To the south, Sequoia and Kings Canyon National Parks. No paved roads enter the forest from the east or south, and only State Route 168 is a major entry point.

Camping Facilities
Camping in this national forest centers around large reservoirs and lakes such as Mammoth Pool, Courtright, and Pine Flat reservoirs, and Huntington, Shaver, and Bass lakes.

Small campgrounds are located along streams away from the popular lakes. These are your best bet if you want a secluded, quiet camping trip where you don't have to worry about how your neighbors are going to act as you try to get the kids to bed at night. Many of these are near enough to the lakes and reservoirs to make a short afternoon trip to swim and laze along the shore a good outing that breaks up the day, but far enough that you may find few others campers in the campground with you.

Many of the more isolated campgrounds in this forest are without running water, but most have some water, such as a mountain stream, nearby. You should always check with the ranger district office about water before heading into one of these isolated campgrounds, though, and carry some sort of water purification apparatus to keep from picking up *Giardia*, the nasty bacteria that disrupts your digestive tract.

Very few of the campgrounds in this national forest are open year-round because most are snowed in during the winter.

Hiking Activities
Hiking is excellent from almost all the campgrounds in this forest. From short hikes along streams and around lakes for the younger kids to longer backcountry hikes into the High Sierra, there is something for everyone. Don't expect self-guided nature trails here, though. You're on your own.

It's a good idea to bring a number of field guides on the subjects that interest you (wildflowers, birds, mammals,

Many lakes and waterways in California are home for wading birds like this resting great blue heron.

tracks, etc.) and make your own nature trails as you hike around the area.

A number of the campgrounds have trails that lead into one of the wilderness areas that take up so much of the national forest here. An overnight outing to a high country lake is a great way to break up the trip for your older children.

Special Outings and Activities
As with all national forests you have to take care of your own special outings, and in this forest they are likely to be associated with water. Whether swimming at one of the many reservoirs and lakes, wading in a mountain stream, or fishing for your dinner, you can find something that interests everyone in the family.

Again, don't expect ranger-led hikes and nightly campfire talks. Most of the campgrounds are just too small and isolated for such amenities. Don't even expect showers. If you need these head for more populated areas where the campgrounds are large enough to warrant them.

STANISLAUS NATIONAL FOREST
Forest Supervisor
19777 Greenley Road
Sonora, CA 95370
(209) 532-3671

This national forest is located in the southern end of the Gold Rush country and is rich in early California history. With elevations between 1,100 and 11,675 feet, and deep canyons cut by four major rivers, the forest offers plenty of variety to visitors.

White-water rafting is popular on an eighteen-mile section of the Tuolumne River with nearly constant white water. The season extends from May through October. Other water sports are available on the 810 miles of streams and 7,000 surface acres of lakes and reservoirs within the forest.

There are four ranger districts with over forty developed campgrounds and three wilderness areas in the million acres of the forest.

Recommended Ages
Good to Excellent for all ages.

Location
The forest is located in the central Sierra Nevada between the Mokelumne and Merced rivers.

Camping Facilities
There are nearly fifty developed campgrounds in this national forest with over 1,000 sites. Only two areas are well developed and crowded, however, and these are the recreation areas at Pinecrest and Alpine lakes.

While the campgrounds in these areas offer all the amenities one could wish for, the rest of the campgrounds in the forest frequently don't even have running water. Although water is generally available from nearby streams or lakes you should be sure to have some way to purify all water before drinking it or using it for cooking.

I like to head for the Sonora Pass area when camping in this forest. There are over twenty campgrounds in this high alpine area. Several of the smaller, more secluded ones on the road to Iceberg Meadow are ideal for any family wishing to get into the high country to camp far from the noisy crowds and to explore the high country on foot.

While the main campground at Pinecrest contains 200 sites, Fence Creek Campground is in an even more scenic area, but it only has 12 sites.

Hiking Activities

Hiking here takes you into high country filled with alpine meadows and cirque lakes. During the summer the meadows are covered with carpets of colorful wildflowers and the lakes provide a great place to soak tired feet for a few minutes. Any longer and you may lose your toes to frostbite because the water is recently melted snow!

Special Outings and Activities

Hiking, fishing, white-water rafting, and lazing under the shade of tall ponderosa pine are about as special as it gets here, and there is plenty of each in this national forest. Don't come here if you want campgrounds with everything from showers to grocery stores. But if you want pleasant weather, beautiful scenery, great hiking, and good fishing it is the place to visit.

TOIYABE NATIONAL FOREST

Forest Supervisor
1200 Franklin Way
Sparks, NV 89431
(702) 331-6444

The Toiyabe National Forest has more land than any other national forest in the lower forty-eight states. Most of it is scattered across large areas of Nevada, but 694,987 acres are located within California.

Within the two ranger districts are some of the most popular recreational areas found in any national forest in California. The campgrounds here range from developed sites in the High Sierra to undeveloped desert sites.

Three wilderness areas are found in these sections of the Toiyabe. They include incredibly scenic regions of the Sierra. A forty-five-mile section of the Pacific Crest Trail cuts through the wilderness areas.

Recommended Ages
Good to Excellent for all ages.

Location
The two ranger districts in California straddle the Nevada–California border in a strip 15 miles wide and almost 100 miles long just south of Lake Tahoe.

Camping Facilities
From Lake Tahoe south along the eastern slope of the Sierra there are twenty-five campgrounds under the jurisdiction of the Carson and Bridgeport ranger districts of the Toiyabe National Forest. These campgrounds are open only during the summer months after the snow melts and the ground dries. This generally means a May through September or October schedule.

Although they are only open a short time each year they are located in an area full of splendor. The eastern slope of the Sierra is much drier than the western slope, and the topography is much steeper. The long western side of the range catches winter storm clouds and gradually pushes them upward until they drop their precipitation as they reach the highest ridges. This leaves the eastern side with a relatively light snowfall and little summer rain.

Whether at campgrounds in the high meadows of the Carson River Valley, in Hope Valley, near Markleeville, or in the higher reaches of the eastern slope above Bridgeport you can find sites near streams and rivers to enjoy some of the finest trout fishing in the state.

These campgrounds are of small to medium size and none have the overdeveloped feeling you often find in the busier regions of the state. You are more likely to encounter hunters and fishermen at these campgrounds than you are campers who have brought their suburban lifestyles with them. There are no boom boxes or big motor homes in these campgrounds. There are only campers who like to get out into the wilderness where they can enjoy what nature has to offer.

Hiking Activities
Trails lead from these campgrounds into high country where the hiking is easy (if you are in shape), and the vistas stretch out over large expanses of the Great Basin Desert to the east. The trails take you to high mountain meadows where wildflowers add a splash of color to the generally gray landscape, and along the shores of small lakes cold from the recent snow melt. Most summers you can find shaded fields of unmelted snow where the kids can slide down the icy surface or glide down on their feet.

Most of the hikes here are for older kids, and few are appropriate for preschoolers. Toddlers and preschoolers do enjoy walking along the banks of the streams and around the shores of the lakes near the campgrounds, however.

Special Outings and Activities
Every outing here is special, but few offer any more than what you get from hiking. Fishing is always good in the streams and lakes, and families with an interest in geology can always take short geology hikes in this geologically active region.

Bird watching is also good, with several rare birds such as the rosy finch found around the higher campgrounds.

YOSEMITE NATIONAL PARK
Superintendent
P.O. Box 577
Yosemite National Park, CA 95389
(209) 372-0264

What can I say about Yosemite that hasn't already been said? Well, for one, there are plenty of spots you can go within the park where you won't be deluged with the noisy crowds in the valley, where most of the millions of visitors congregate. In the less-visited portions of the park you can hike along trails where you are more likely to encounter a bear than you are another person, and in the higher elevations you will find some of the best alpine flower blooms in the state.

There are seven campgrounds with 825 campsites in the valley, and ten campgrounds with over 1,000 sites outside the valley but within the park boundaries.

Only 35 miles of hiking trails crisscross the valley floor, but over 750 miles cover vast areas that see little use outside the valley.

Recommended Ages
Excellent for all ages.

Location
The park is located in the central Sierra Nevada to the east of Merced and the Central Valley. Both State Routes 120 and 140 lead to the park.

Camping Facilities
Without reservation I recommend that you find a campground outside the valley floor on any visit to Yosemite. Not only are they less developed and less crowded, they are also located in extremely scenic areas. For all the valley floor has to offer, it just can't match the scenery found in Tuolumne Meadows and other locations along Tioga Road.

It's a long drive, but if you must visit the valley floor you can do so as a day outing. You can then return to the clear air and quiet times found at the campgrounds away from the valley.

One problem is that you can make reservations for sites within the valley, but all the campgrounds outside the valley are on a first-come, first-served basis. If you reach the campgrounds late on a Sunday or early on a Monday, however, you should have no problem finding a site.

Hiking Activities

Hiking is what the higher regions of Yosemite are all about. Great trails lead across meadows carpeted with alpine wildflowers, to the top of domes from which you can see great granite outcroppings shaped by glaciers and erosion, and into groves of pine where the bird life is active during the brief summer.

In the valley there are a number of short trails that are excellent for preschoolers and several strenuous hikes to the top of falls for older youngsters.

Special Outings and Activities

Waterfalls, granite domes, and rushing mountain streams all add to the attraction of this popular national park. Kids have a full range of activities led by rangers, from a Junior Ranger program to special nature walks, and always enjoy the campfire talks given by the rangers at night.

If you head for the valley floor don't expect quiet and solitude. Instead you will find traffic congestion, noise, foul air, and long lines. But you will also get the incomparable beauty of the granite walls carved by long gone glaciers and the waterfalls that drop from hanging valleys above.

CHAPTER · 5

SOUTH COAST CAMPING

ong white sand beaches come to mind when Southern California camping is mentioned, but the region's coastal hills that rise abruptly from the shore also offer great camping. The beaches and hills offer some of the best camping in the state from late fall through late spring.

While there is not the great geographical diversity found in the inland regions, the weather is spectacular most of the winter. And who doesn't like sunny weather, warm oceans, and great hiking in the hills above, where views to all four points of the compass are outstanding.

The Santa Monica Mountains National Recreation Area provides plenty of outdoor activities for residents of the Los Angeles Basin, and it extends westward all the way to the ocean. All the camping in the recreation area is located in several state park units within its boundaries, and these have been included as separate entries.

ANGELES NATIONAL FOREST
Forest Supervisor
701 North Santa Anita Avenue
Arcadia, CA 91006
(818) 574-5200

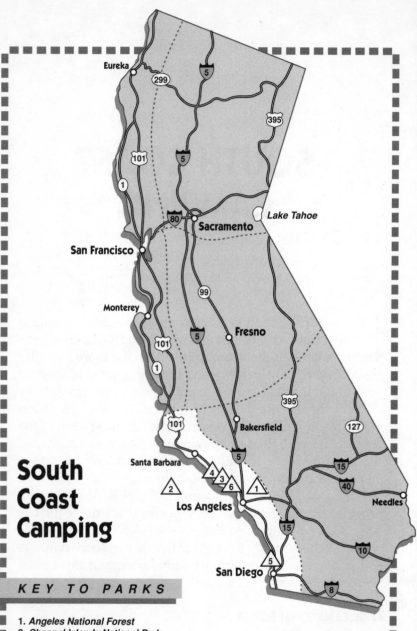

South Coast Camping

KEY TO PARKS

1. *Angeles National Forest*
2. *Channel Islands National Park*
3. *Leo Carillo State Beach*
4. *Point Magu State Park*
5. *San Diego State Beaches*
6. *Topanga State Park*

This 693,000-acre national forest is the prime recreational area for the residents of the Los Angeles area. From the gentle, wildflower-covered slopes in the Saugus District to the desert terrain of the Tujunga and Valyermo districts there are hundreds of miles of hiking trails that offer great opportunities for day and overnight hikes. These include a long section of the Pacific Crest Trail.

Three wilderness areas are located in the five ranger districts. Developed campgrounds are spread throughout the forest and are popular Southern California destinations year-round.

Recommended Ages
Good to Excellent for all ages.

Location
This national forest lies just to the north of the Los Angeles Basin and extends from Ventura County in the west to San Bernardino County in the east.

Camping Facilities
Over fifty campgrounds are scattered through the vast expanses of this national forest that covers some of the most scenic areas of Southern California. From the rolling hills around Saugus, with large reservoirs such as Castaic and Pyramid lakes, to the top of peaks such as Mt. Baldy in the San Gabriel Mountains, campgrounds in the Angeles National Forest provide great natural getaways.

A popular campground in the Mt. Baldy area is the 176-site Crystal Lake Campground. A large visitor center here provides information about the smaller campgrounds in the district, such as Manker Flats, a twenty-site campground that sits at 6,300 feet where the climate is good from early spring through late fall.

The Big Pines Recreation Area, with over a dozen small to medium campgrounds at 6,000 feet and above, is a good place to go during the midsummer heat waves that hit Southern

California. Here you can camp alongside mountain streams under tall pines while the rest of the region swelters in 100-degree-plus temperatures.

The most developed campground in this area is the 115-site Table Mountain Campground at 7,000 feet. The Big Pines Visitor Center is nearby, and if you have not camped in this area before you should head for Table Mountain and investigate the smaller campgrounds on your first visit. You can then find which one best suits your needs for return visits.

Another popular camping area is the Arroyo Seco Ranger District to the west of the San Gabriel Wilderness. A number of campgrounds are located above 5,000 feet in pine forests within an easy drive of San Bernardino. The Angeles Crest and Angeles Forest highways take you to forest service roads that lead into the backcountry and to Chilao Campground, with 115 sites, which is at least partially open year-round. There is another large visitor center located near this campground where you can find out more about the less-developed areas of the ranger district.

Hiking Activities

Good, well-maintained trails lead out from almost all of the campgrounds in this national forest, and a large section of the Pacific Crest Trail runs through the forest near the Big Pines Recreation Area. Several short nature trails are also located there, which kids like to use to learn about the natural history of the region.

Special Outings and Activities

Fishing and swimming are great in the reservoirs of the Saugus Ranger District, which also offer opportunity for other water sports such as boating and waterskiing.

As you head farther west to the Tujunga and Valyermo ranger districts, hikes lead through exposed rocks reflecting the tremendous geological forces that shaped the region. The San Gabriel Mountains, thought to be the most geologically active mountains in the world, are continuing to grow at a steady rate and you can see the results of that movement as you hike along the trails.

During the spring, wildflowers provide brilliant displays on the hills of the Saugus District that draw thousands of visitors. Campers can walk through these from a number of campgrounds.

CHANNEL ISLANDS NATIONAL PARK
Superintendent
1901 Spinnaker Drive
Ventura, CA 93001
(805) 644-8262

This national park is unusual in that the only access to it is by boat. Five channel islands off the coast of California to the west of Ventura are included in the national park. Two are still privately owned, but you can visit the rest: Anacapa, San Miguel, and Santa Barbara.

These islands, which are more than ten miles from Oxnard and Ventura, are rookeries for gulls, cormorants, brown pelicans, and other sea birds, as well as haul-out points for sea lions and harbor seals. The annual gray whale migration also passes close by Anacapa Island.

Primitive camping is allowed on Anacapa and Santa Barbara islands but all campers must bring their own water. The visitor center is located onshore in Ventura, and it is there that you obtain permits, maps, and other information about where to camp and what to do on the islands.

The authorized park concessionaire boat service to the islands is Island Packers, 1867 Spinnaker Drive, Ventura, CA 93001; reservations: (805) 642-1393, information: (805) 642-7688.

Recommended Ages
Poor for toddlers and preschoolers, Excellent for 6–9 and for 10 and over.

Location
In the Pacific Ocean off the coast from Oxnard and Ventura. You

can either take your own boat to these islands or use the ferries of Island Packers, the park concessionaire. Their number is (805) 642-1393 for reservations, or (805) 642-7688 for information.

Camping Facilities
Primitive camping is allowed only on Anacapa and Santa Barbara islands, and camping is restricted to designated areas.

The camping facilities are so primitive that you must bring all your own water, fuel for cooking, and other supplies. There are no supplies on the islands, but the designated camping areas do have pit toilets, tables, and fire grills. The latter cannot be used between May and October, or during other extremely dry periods.

The campground on Anacapa Island is near the small ranger station. Also nearby are the Anacapa Island lighthouse, several nice coves, and a haul-out spot for California sea lions. The only other island in the group where camping is allowed is Santa Barbara, a small island on the southern end of the chain. With only 640 acres, there is not a lot to do on Santa Barbara, but there is a small campground near the landing cove. Again, you must bring your own water and supplies to both of these campgrounds because there are no developed facilities at them.

Since you must bring all your equipment and supplies in by boat, here are a couple of suggestions that will make your visit more successful. One, limit what you take to absolute necessities since you will have to carry everything from the landing platform to the camping area. Two, pack everything in easily handled backpacks or duffel bags. You must unload from a skiff and pass your baggage up a ladder before carrying it to the camp areas, which are a quarter- and a half-mile from the landing platforms.

One other suggestion. There is generally a stiff wind on the island; you will sleep more comfortably if you have a tent to deflect the wind at night.

Hiking Activities

Although Santa Barbara is small there are over five miles of trails that crisscross the marine terrace and lead to the top of two peaks. The trails also take you to the Santa Barbara Island lighthouse, Cave Canyon, a sea lion rookery, and Elephant Seal Cove. Be sure to take the self-guiding nature trail near the ranger station before heading out onto the rest of the trails. It will teach you about the natural history of the island and the kids will have a good idea of what to expect as they move around the island.

On Anacapa Island, which is really three small islets, there are fewer trails because West Anacapa is closed to visitors to protect a pelican rookery. There is a short self-guiding nature trail near the visitor center and ranger station on East Anacapa, but you can hike over large areas of East and Middle Anacapa islands if you have a boat to take you from island to island.

Special Outings and Activities

In addition to bird watching and visiting sea lion and seal rookeries and haul-outs there is little to do on these islands.

A female elephant seal relaxes on the beach.

If you have a boat there are several excellent scuba and snorkeling areas just offshore Anacapa.

You may want to spend time sitting on high points looking for gray whale, Pacific white-sided dolphin, or the great blue whale, the largest creature on earth, which feeds offshore.

If you head for the islands during early spring you will find fields carpeted with coreopsis, morning glories, and mallow, and if you are truly lucky you may see a tiny island fox searching for a nest with eggs or young hatchlings.

This is a park you head for when you want to spend some time in true wilderness without spending a lot of time and energy getting there.

LEO CARILLO STATE BEACH
1925 Las Virgenes
Calabasas, CA 91302
(818) 880-0350

This 1,602-acre park has 1.5 miles of beach and uplands where the elevations reach 1,500 feet. Swimming, fishing, beachcombing, and hiking are favorite activities here.

Recommended Ages
Good to Excellent for all ages.

Location
The park is on the Pacific Coast, twenty-eight miles northwest of Santa Monica off State Route 1.

Camping Facilities
There are two campgrounds with 188 developed sites in this park. The largest campground, and the most desirable to me, is the 138-site campground that sits in a canyon across State Route 1 from the beach. The sites here offer some seclusion from your neighbors, so you don't have the infusion of day use visitors each morning to disturb your quiet. The 50-site beach campground is more open and there is no privacy.

Both campgrounds accommodate trailers and motor

homes to thirty-one feet, and showers are scattered around the campgrounds.

The campgrounds are open year-round and on the State Park Reservation System March through November.

Hiking Activities

A quarter-mile-long, self-guiding nature trail circles the campfire center at the far end of the canyon campground. This is a good hike for toddlers and preschoolers, and older kids enjoy learning about the natural history of the area before heading out on a longer hike along the bluffs near the ocean or up into the hills behind the campground on the Yellowhill Fire Trail.

Special Outings and Activities

Swimming, fishing, and sunning yourself on the beach are special activities here. By far, most campers come for the beach and associated activities. On summer weekends and major holidays the beach is packed. This keeps me away, but some families enjoy the excitement of the crowds.

I prefer to head for such beach campgrounds when the weather is a little cooler and the crowds are gone. Then I can walk along the beach without having to pick my way through a barrier of beach blankets and coolers. Birds are out then, and I may see seals, sea lions, otters, or whales offshore.

This park is part of the Santa Monica Mountains National Recreation Area, and over thirty organizations lead groups, give classes, and otherwise provide families an opportunity to enjoy learning about the natural history of the area. Contact the recreation headquarters at Santa Monica Mountains National Recreation Area, 22900 Ventura Boulevard, Suite 140, Woodland Hills, CA 91364; (213) 888-3770, for more information about the many activities available.

POINT MUGU STATE PARK
1925 Las Virgenes
Calabasas, CA 91302
(818) 880-0350

A number of parks along the south coast offer equestrian campgrounds for those who want to explore the area on horseback.

More than seventy miles of hiking and horseback riding trails crisscross this 14,980-acre park. With some five miles of shoreline, sandy beaches, rocky bluffs, and a spectacular sand dune there is plenty to enjoy near the coast, but don't forget to head inland where two major canyons with grassy valley floors cut through rugged terrain. Equestrians come to this park for the trail rides and the two equestrian camping areas.

Recommended Ages
Excellent for all ages.

Location
The park is fifteen miles south of Oxnard on State Route 1 at the western end of the Santa Monica Mountains.

Camping Facilities
There are fifty developed sites at Big Sycamore Campground near the park headquarters, where there are showers and sites that accommodate thirty-one-foot trailers and motor homes.

Several miles up the Pacific Coast Highway (State Route 1) the La Jolla Beach Campground has 100 primitive sites that are primarily used by campers and those with motor homes up to thirty-one feet. There are no showers here. There is a walk-in campground in La Jolla Valley which is two miles via La Jolla Canyon Trail or five miles via Sycamore Canyon Trail.

This park also has two equestrian camping areas. These can handle up to seventy-five horses and have water troughs. You can trailer to these sites from Newbury Park.

The campgrounds are open year-round and on the State Park Reservation System March through November.

Hiking Activities

More than seventy-five miles of hiking and horseback riding trails are located within the park boundaries, and over a thousand miles of trails are part of the Santa Monica Mountains National Recreation Area. This large recreation area surrounds Point Mugu and several other state and county parks in the area.

Short trails appropriate for toddlers and preschoolers lead out from Sycamore Canyon Campground, and longer trails take you into the dense chaparral country above the ocean.

Special Outings and Activities

Children like to come to this park for the swimming and beach-related activities, and there is some fishing for those so inclined. There are nature exhibits at the park headquarters, and rangers lead hikes during the day. Campfire talks are given nightly during the busy season.

See the entry for Leo Carillo State Beach (page 186) for information about the many organizations that provide classes and outings for families and children in the Santa Monica Mountains National Recreation Area.

SAN DIEGO STATE BEACHES
2680 Carlsbad Boulevard
Carlsbad, CA 92008
(619) 729-8947

Of the seven units of state beaches near San Diego two provide camping. These sit atop bluffs with views of the beaches and ocean where surfers ride the waves. South Carlsbad and San Elijo state beaches both have campgrounds, and along with the other five are among the most popular state parks in California.

Recommended Ages
Excellent for all ages.

Location
South Carlsbad State Beach is located on Carlsbad Boulevard three miles south of Carlsbad and San Elijo State Beach is located on old U.S. 101 between the small communities of Encinitas and Cardiff-by-the-Sea.

Camping Facilities
San Elijo State Beach has 171 developed sites with showers. The sites accommodate thirty-five-foot trailers and motor homes. South Carlsbad State Beach has 222 developed sites with showers, and also accommodates thirty-five-foot trailers and motor homes.

Both of these are extremely popular campgrounds that are open all year. San Elijo is on the State Park Reservation System January through November, and South Carlsbad from mid-March through December.

Hiking Activities
Hiking near both of these campgrounds is limited, but kids like to hike along the bluffs and sand dunes and beachcomb along the shoreline when the crowds are small.

Special Outings and Activities
Water related sports such as swimming, fishing, boogie boarding, and playing in the sand are special here. If you don't want the sun and surf, head for a campground inland. These are strictly for those who like the ocean.

TOPANGA STATE PARK
1925 Las Virgenes
Calabasas, CA 91302
(818) 880-0350

This park is the second-largest urban park in the country, and the world's largest wildland found within the boundaries of a major city. Most of its 9,181 acres lie within the Los Angeles city limits. Over thirty miles of trails traverse the rugged terrain of the park. The most popular attraction within the park is the Trippet Ranch self-guided nature trail.

Camping here is restricted to eight sites at a hike-in camp and a group site that handles twenty-five people.

Recommended Ages
Poor for toddlers and preschoolers, Excellent for 6–9 and for 10 and over.

Location
The park is on Topanga Boulevard from State Routes 1 and 27.

Camping Facilities
Camping facilities are limited in this state park, but if you live nearby it is a good place to introduce your kids to backpacking without having to drive hundreds of miles to find out they don't really like it.

Hiking Activities
Hiking is great in this park and the surrounding Santa Monica Mountains National Recreation Area. Most of this is for older kids, though, and you have to search for areas where preschoolers and toddlers can enjoy a hike.

Special Outings and Activities
See the Leo Carillo State Beach entry (page 186) for information on organizations that provide classes and outings for families and children in the Santa Monica Mountains National Recreation Area.

CHAPTER · 6

SOUTH INLAND CAMPING

When I head for the deserts of Southern California I'm looking for warm weather, cloudless skies, and brilliant stands of wildflowers. These are a great relief to me living as I do in the rainy climes of the North Coast where winter skies are leaden covers that reach lower and lower until I feel claustrophobic. This unbroken cover can hover overhead for weeks at a time, and often it is broken only by a downpour that continues for more weeks.

That is the time to head for the Providence Mountains, Joshua Tree National Park, and Anza-Borrego Desert State Park where the winds may be brisk but the skies so clear as to seem transparent. Night skies reveal stars not seen for months in the north, and hikes through open desert lead past the renewal of life as the small wildflowers that carpet the openings between green cacti break through the desert soil after the winter rains.

While the camping here is unsurpassed between early fall and late spring, summers become unbearable with temperatures above 100 degrees most days. The desert is not a pleasant place to camp with children then. That is when you head to the small mountain ranges that rise as much as 12,000 feet above the desert floor. There you can find campgrounds

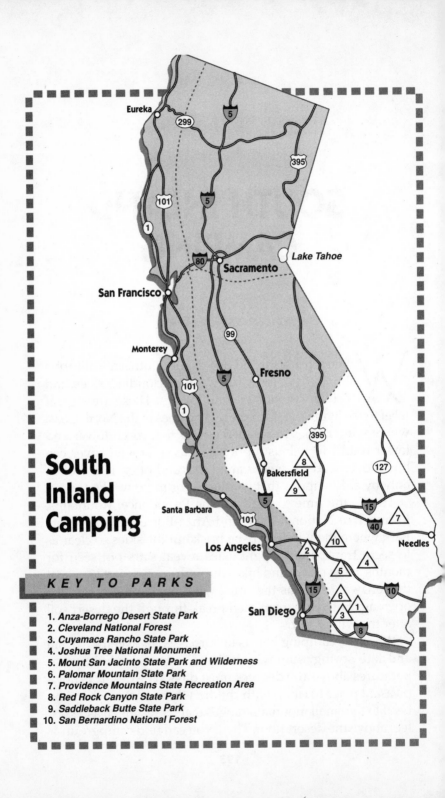

South
Inland
Camping

KEY TO PARKS

1. *Anza-Borrego Desert State Park*
2. *Cleveland National Forest*
3. *Cuyamaca Rancho State Park*
4. *Joshua Tree National Monument*
5. *Mount San Jacinto State Park and Wilderness*
6. *Palomar Mountain State Park*
7. *Providence Mountains State Recreation Area*
8. *Red Rock Canyon State Park*
9. *Saddleback Butte State Park*
10. *San Bernardino National Forest*

Eureka

Sacramento
Lake Tahoe
San Francisco
Monterey
Fresno
Bakersfield
Santa Barbara
Los Angeles
Needles
San Diego

nestled among tall conifers. These conifer forests aren't as lush as those found in the Sierra forests, but their open understory makes hiking and exploration easy.

Several reservoirs in the region offer water sports activities and have large campgrounds that are full most of the year as people escape from the large population centers of Southern California to a semblance of wilderness.

ANZA-BORREGO DESERT STATE PARK
200 Palm Canyon Drive
Borrego Springs, CA 92004
(619) 767-5311

Over 500 miles of primitive roads lead to the far reaches of this enormous state park. With over 600,000 acres, the park has half the total acreage of the California State Park System and is the largest state park in the nation. Although it has only two developed campgrounds, this is the only state park in California where you can camp outside designated areas.

Most visitors avoid the park during midsummer when the temperatures regularly exceed 100 degrees, but plenty flock

Spring flowers add color to the green of new grass.

there in early spring when the desert wildflowers are in full bloom.

Recommended Ages
Poor for toddlers, Good for preschoolers, Excellent for 6–9 and for 10 and over.

Location
The park is about eighty-five miles northeast of San Diego off I-8 on State Routes 78 and 79.

Camping Facilities
Despite its size this park has very limited developed camping. Borrego Palm Canyon has sixty-five developed sites for tents, twenty-four-foot trailers, and thirty-one-foot motor homes, and fifty-two sites with full hook-ups for thirty-five-foot trailers and motor homes. Solar showers are located throughout the campground. Tamarisk Grove Campground has twenty-five developed sites that accommodate twenty-one-foot trailers and motor homes. It also has solar showers.

Although you may camp anywhere within the park, there are also ten primitive camping areas scattered throughout the park with pit toilets and tables. None of these has water, though.

There are also ten equestrian camping areas with corrals and water. There is plenty of trailer space and primitive sites for twenty-four-foot trailers and motor homes.

Hiking Activities
Hiking up desert canyons, through fields of desert wildflowers, and along mountain ridges is available in this huge park. This is one of the best places in the nation for desert hiking, and a great place to introduce children to this exciting activity. You may want to begin with the nature trail at Borrego Palm Canyon and then spread out to explore other regions of the park.

If the temperatures begin to climb above the century mark

you will want to head for the higher elevations of the park, because most kids don't do well hiking in hot weather. Neither do most parents, for that matter.

Special Outings and Activities
People head to this large park to explore its fragile and unfamiliar desert environment. In the winter you can watch migrating birds, in the spring there are desert wildflowers to hike through, and in the fall you can enjoy the cool days and cold, clear nights found only in the desert. Smart parents don't head for the park with kids in the summer because the temperatures are just too high for anyone to truly enjoy a camping trip.

Two special events at the park are the annual Native American Days held the first weekend in February and Earth Day in the Desert in late April. Native American Days celebrate the lifestyles of Southern California tribes who survived and flourished in the desert for centuries before the United States was formed. As many as 5,000 people make the trek to the desert for this two-day event. Earth Day in the Desert includes speakers, presentations, exhibits, and family activities at the park visitor center, a unique building that is partially buried and nearly indistinguishable from the surrounding desert environment.

CLEVELAND NATIONAL FOREST
Forest Supervisor
10845 Rancho Bernardo Road, Suite 200
San Diego, CA 92127-2107
(619) 673-6180

This national forest is divided into three separate units in San Diego, Orange, and Riverside counties. In the southern unit, boulder-strewn hills are thickly covered with chaparral, while the upper units have mile-high mountains where conifer forests cover flat plateaus. Four wilderness areas are found in the almost 600,000 acres of the forest.

This is a fragile forest where wildfires are common due to

the hot, dry weather that makes the forest a tinderbox in late summer and early fall. Because of fire dangers open fires are restricted in the forest all year.

Recommended Ages
Good to Excellent for all ages.

Location
The units of the forests extend from about five miles north of the Mexican border to the edge of the Los Angeles Basin.

Camping Facilities
The campgrounds in this national forest are in the hills along-side I-15 and State Routes 78 and 79 as they follow the ridge of mountains that separate the southern coast of Orange and San Diego counties from the desert inland.

The campgrounds in the Trabuco Ranger District are south-west of Lake Elsinore, a popular water sports center in the region. Four of the five campgrounds in the district are located off State Route 74 (Ortega Highway) and Long Canyon Road. These are easily accessible and fill quickly during the busy season. Only Tenaja Campground is difficult to reach, as it is located at the end of twelve miles of dirt road. Even its five sites fill during midseason, but other times it offers a good place to head if you want to stay in the Southern California mountains but want to get away from the noisy crowds generally found near water sports hot spots.

Five medium-sized campgrounds of twenty to ninety sites are located near the Palomar Observatory high in the Palomar Mountains. There you can find a bit of the Sierra in Southern California, but you may have to reserve a site if you want to enjoy the cool, pine-sheltered campgrounds during the summer.

Farther south there are two larger campgrounds, Burnt Rancheria with 108 sites and Laguna with 105, just north of I-8 to the east of San Diego. Along with three smaller campgrounds these are popular camping sites for San Diegans and surrounding suburbia residents. While they offer a good opportunity to enjoy wild country close by a major metropolitan area, they also fill quickly on summer weekends.

You can make reservation for sites in most of the campgrounds in this heavily used national forest. During fall and winter the nights are too cool for many families, so if your family is hardy you can find good sites with few neighbors almost any weekend.

Hiking Activities
As with most national forests hiking is a prime way to explore the countryside surrounding the campgrounds. From short hikes along streams and around lakes to longer hikes up peaks with vistas that stretch for miles in all four directions, there are hikes for all ages here. Summer hiking can be enervating in the heat of Southern California, even at higher elevations, so be sure everyone has enough to drink as you explore the region.

Special Outings and Activities
You'll need to make your own special outings. Find a good bird watching spot, look for signs of large mammals (cougars, deer, and coyote are plentiful in the region), or just laze under the shade of tall trees.

CUYAMACA RANCHO STATE PARK
12551 Highway 79
Descanso, CA 91916
(619) 765-0755

Over half of the 24,677 acres in this park are classified as wilderness where no vehicles, including mountain bikes, are allowed. Elevations in the park range from 4,000 to 6,512 feet, and beautiful pine and oak forests cover the rugged hills and broad meadows. Small streams run through many areas of the park. The region is rich in both human and natural history, and a museum near park headquarters tells of the natives who lived here for centuries.

While long hikes may seem to take you away
from civilization, you can often view it in the
distance at many parks.

The forests are home to over 300 species of birds that have
been seen in the park, and mountain lions roam the hills,
sometimes coming into the campgrounds. Although there
have been several attacks on humans, primarily youngsters,
in the past decade, danger from the lions is minimal if you
follow the precautions laid out by park rangers.

Recommended Ages
Excellent for all ages.

Location
The park is nine miles north of I-8 on State Route 79 to the
east of San Diego.

Camping Facilities

Two large developed campgrounds, eighty-five-site Paso Picacho and eighty-one-site Green Valley, accommodate trailers and motor homes to thirty feet and have amenities such as showers and trailer sanitation stations.

Although the sites in Paso Picacho are less secluded than those in Green Valley, I recommend Paso Picacho because of the number of nearby trails that children can use. The park's interpretive center is located near the entrance to this campground.

There are sixteen developed family equestrian sites at Los Caballos Campground. Water troughs and metal corrals are provided at this trailer-in campground. There are primitive trail camps for equestrians at Arroyo Seco and Granite Springs, where corrals and water troughs are provided.

The family campgrounds are open and on the State Park Reservation System year-round, and the Los Caballos Campground is open all year and on the State Park Reservation System mid-May through October.

Hiking Activities

Hiking is a favorite activity in this wilderness park, and there are over 100 miles of trails that lead from the campgrounds into the back country. There is also a short nature trail at the Paso Picacho Campground that gives detailed information about the natural history of the region. Even toddlers and preschoolers enjoy this short hike. The slightly longer Azalea Glen Loop Trail is good for advanced preschoolers and older children as it loops around the campground.

For a great day outing with older kids take the 3.5-mile long Cuyamaca Peak Trail from the Paso Picacho Campground. This moderately strenuous hike culminates at the top of the 6,512-foot peak where you have spectacular views of the ocean to the west, the desert to the east, and Mexico and the Salton Sea to the south and east.

Special Outings and Activities

Several outings here offer kids a chance to understand more

about the human history of the region. One is the exhibit at the Stonewall Mine site. A pictorial history here depicts life and activities at the greatest of Southern California gold mines. Another is the exhibit of the region's plants and animals at the park's interpretive center. Finally, a museum at the park headquarters tells the story of the Native Americans who lived here for centuries before the Europeans arrived.

For those who like to drop a line in the water to see if there is anything biting, several small streams in the park offer moderate fishing.

JOSHUA TREE NATIONAL MONUMENT
Superintendent
74485 National Monument Drive
Twentynine Palms, CA 92277-3597
(619) 367-7511

The Colorado and Mojave deserts merge in this large desert park. Nowhere else in California can you see the contrast between high and low deserts so vividly. Tree-sized yuccas known as Joshua trees dominate the vegetation of the higher and wetter areas of the park, and visitors flock to the region for the wildflower displays in the spring.

Summers are hot, although more moderate, at the higher elevations: The region averages over seventy-five days a year when the temperature exceeds 100 degrees. The campgrounds in the park are located between 3,000 and 4,500 feet, and even during the summer are pleasant places to camp.

Recommended Ages
Poor for toddlers, Good for preschoolers, Excellent for 6–9 and for 10 and over.

Location
The park is about 140 miles east of Los Angeles, and approaches to its north and south entrances are off I-10.

Camping Facilities

There are nine campgrounds in the park with 535 sites. These are developed campgrounds with tables, fire pits, and pit toilets, but only Cottonwood near the southern entrance has piped water. In all the others you must provide your own.

Most of the campgrounds are located among the large boulder fields that dot the upper regions of the park, and children like to crawl around on the boulders near their sites. My favorite is Jumbo Rocks Campground, but you really can't miss at any of them.

Equestrian camping is allowed at Ryan and Black Rock campgrounds, with the latter exclusively for equestrian use. It is also the only one with water.

All family campsites are on a first-come, first-served basis, and some are closed in midsummer.

Backcountry camping is allowed with permits, but you must pack your own water. I would try this only with older kids.

Hiking Activities

Hiking is excellent here. The trails are open, and only lightly used, and there are literally dozens to choose from. The park provides an information sheet of the marked and maintained trails in the park and you can pick one up at any of the three visitor centers (Twenty-Nine Palms Oasis, Indian Cove, and Cottonwood).

In addition to the backcountry trails there are nine self-guiding interpretive trails located throughout the park along the roads. These provide you with an opportunity to explore the various types of vegetation that thrive in the high desert environment without your going too far afield.

For those who want to drive and walk, there is an eighteen-mile-long self-guiding motor tour of the various regions of the park. You can pick up a brochure at the visitor centers. On this tour you can stop at many of the self-guiding interpretive trails for short walks into the desert.

Special Outings and Activities
Visiting the desert in its primeval beauty is the special outing here, and you can learn more about it by stopping at a visitor center and looking at the exhibits. These also direct you to the wayside exhibits that are located along the highway at various sites in the park. During fall and spring, when the campgrounds are more heavily used, rangers lead hikes and talks on weekends.

A very special treat for many is the glorious display of wildflowers that carpet the desert floor in early spring. These are especially colorful after wet winters. A walk up any wash or canyon takes you through areas of profuse blooms.

MOUNT SAN JACINTO STATE PARK AND WILDERNESS
17801 Lake Perris Drive
Perris, CA 92370
(714) 659-2607

Granite peaks, pine forests, and mountain meadows are all found in this wilderness park. Mt. San Jacinto is one of only five peaks in Southern California that exceeds 10,000 feet in elevation.

There are both primitive and developed campgrounds in the park, as well as hike-in campsites for those who wish to experience the wilderness overnight.

The area is administered by both the California Department of Parks and Recreation and the U.S. Forest Service.

Recommended Ages
Poor for toddlers, Good for preschoolers, Excellent for 6–9 and for 10 and over.

Location
The park is on State Route 243 near Idyllwild adjacent to the wilderness area.

Camping Facilities
The state park operates two campgrounds in the region, Idyll-

wild Campground with 33 developed sites with showers and Stone Creek with 50 primitive sites with no showers. The forest service operates four others nearby. These add another 102 sites.

All of these campgrounds are above 5,000 feet and offer great escapes from Southern California summers. Unfortunately, many people know about them so you must reserve early for a summer weekend. The forest service campgrounds are on a first-come, first-served basis so you may find an empty site early in the week.

They are also less likely to be full in early spring and in the fall after school has begun. They offer great camping during those times and a long weekend will give you a chance for either an early start on the camping season or a final outing before winter sets in.

Hiking Activities

A short nature trail near Idyllwild Campground is a great way to introduce the kids to the natural history of the region, and longer trails lead into the wilderness area beyond.

Older kids enjoy the longer hikes, particularly those to Suicide Rock and Tahquiz Peak Lookout. You can hike as far as you like into the wilderness area, and can obtain a permit to camp overnight at one of the four designated hike-in campsites.

Special Outings and Activities

The campgrounds here are more like forest service campgrounds where you have to design your own special outings and activities. Hiking is the primary activity chosen by most families.

One outing children like is to drive around to Palm Springs and the Palm Springs Aerial Tramway. The 2.5-mile-long tram ride takes you from 2,643 feet at the Valley Station to 8,516 feet at the Mountain Station on the side of the mountain at the edge of the wilderness area. Children frequently enjoy this ride more than adults. The tram deposits you high on the slopes of the mountain and you can hike the two-mile-long Desert View Trail near the Mountain Station after visiting the Long Valley Ranger Station. Or you can go as far as you're able up the six miles of trail that lead to the top of Mt. San Jacinto, then head back down to the tram and then to the valley floor.

PALOMAR MOUNTAIN STATE PARK
19952 State Park Road
Palomar Mountain, CA 92060
(619) 742-3462

This is one of the few places in Southern California that offers a Sierra-like atmosphere. Summer evenings are cool and the days are pleasant under a canopy of large fir, pine, and cedar trees. The 1,897-acre park's average elevation is 5,500 feet.

Recommended Ages
Good for toddlers and preschoolers, Excellent for 6–9 and for 10 and over.

Location
The park is off State Route 76 to the northeast of Escondido.

Camping Facilities
Doane Valley Campground has thirty-one developed sites that accommodate trailers and motor homes to twenty-one feet, and showers are located throughout the campground. The campground is open and on the State Park Reservation System year-round.

Hiking Activities
A short nature trail leads from the campground to Doane Pond, and kids like to walk along it learning about the natural history of the region. Longer hikes take you to sites such as Scott's Cabin, the park headquarters, the Silver Crest Picnic Area and Observation Point, and Boucher Lookout and Observation Point. Along these trails you'll occasionally catch a glimpse of the Pacific Ocean to the west.

None of these trails is too difficult for advanced preschoolers and older children, and even toddlers enjoy the nature trail.

Special Outings and Activities
Doane Pond is stocked with trout early in the year, and fishing is good from midwinter through early summer. After that the kids like to fish for pan fish such as blue gill and perch. Swimming isn't good in the pond, but kids do like to explore around its edges for small aquatic animals.

Scott's Cabin is a historic site where kids can learn about early settlers of the region from the displays at the cabin.

PROVIDENCE MOUNTAINS STATE RECREATION AREA
14651 Cedar Circle
Hesperia, CA 92345
(619) 389-2281

Limestone caverns with intricate formations are the feature of this 5,250-acre park. Mitchell Caverns Natural Preserve is the most popular cavern, but visitors can take more rustic tours of El Pakiva and Tecopa caverns.

While most visitors come for the caverns, there are several trails within the recreation area that offer spectacular views of the surrounding mountains and desert.

The East Mojave Natural Preserve surrounds this small state park, and several primitive campgrounds now run by the National Park Service are located nearby.

Recommended Ages
Poor for toddlers, Good for preschoolers, Excellent for 6–9 and for 10 and over.

Location
The recreation area is located seventeen miles north of I-40 on Essex Road.

Camping Facilities
Only six primitive sites are located in the state recreation area.

These have no showers and accommodate trailers and motor homes to thirty-one feet.

Within twenty-five miles are two other primitive campgrounds, Hole-in-the-Wall and Mid Hills, each with about twenty primitive sites. They also are without showers and accommodate trailers and motor homes to about thirty feet.

The views from Mid Hills are some of the best found in the East Mojave as you look out over the Cima Dome region, as well as Wild Horse Mesa of Zane Grey fame.

The campgrounds are open year-round, but may be closed because of snow at times during the cold winter months.

Hiking Activities

At the state recreation area marked and maintained trails lead to Crystal Spring and El Pakiva and Tecopa caves. These are moderate trails that even young children can handle, but for the very young take the Mary Beal Nature Trail from the visitor center. This short trail is a self-guiding nature trail that introduces the plants and animals of the East Mojave.

Between Mid Hills and Hole-in-the-Wall campgrounds is an eight-mile trail that leads through wild desert country, where you may hear coyote at night and see small fox during early morning and evening hours.

The terrain around the caverns is rugged and covered with pinon pine and juniper, so hiking is strenuous after you leave the several marked trails. Around the two other campgrounds the land is open and it is easy to hike to nearby mesas and canyons without worrying about getting lost. There you can choose just how far you want to hike without concern about marked trails.

Kids like to head out from the Hole-in-the-Wall Campground to the trail to Mid Hills because they must climb down a narrow passage of weathered volcanic rock to begin the hike. The passage is so steep that hikers must use iron rings that were installed years ago as handholds. These assist in both ascending and descending the narrow passage. Very young children have a hard time making the climb, but children preschool age and above can make the climb easily.

Special Outings and Activities

The tours of the caverns are the special outing here, and kids especially like to tour the caverns without electric lights and paved pathways.

Nighttime star gazing is also a favorite activity in this area far from the city lights and polluted atmosphere of metropolitan Southern California.

RED ROCK CANYON STATE PARK

RRC, Box 26
Cantil, CA 93519
(805) 942-0662

This park is a photographer's dream. The colors of the canyon walls range from stark white to vivid red to dark brown. The spectacular rock formations in the canyons are also pleasant to hike through most of the year, but summers can be very hot. Fall through spring are the best times to visit this high desert park, and winters can be cold to frigid so be prepared.

Only foot travel is permitted in the two natural areas in the park. This makes it a haven from the off-road vehicles that challenge hikers in many desert areas.

Recommended Ages

Poor for toddlers and preschoolers, Excellent for 6–9 and for 10 and over.

Location

The park is twenty-five miles northeast of Mojave on State Route 14.

Camping Facilities

The fifty primitive sites here accommodate thirty-foot trailers and motor homes. There are no showers, although there is piped water. The campground is open and on a first-come, first-served basis year-round.

Cholla cacti and Joshua trees cover large portions of the Mojave Desert.

Hiking Activities

From the short, self-guiding nature trail that begins near the campground to longer hikes that take you into the Red Cliffs and Hagen natural preserves, there is excellent hiking for all ages in this park. Older kids particularly like the fantastic rock formations found in the canyons.

This is wild desert country and you should be aware of all the rules for desert survival. Make sure younger children do not wonder far from the rest of the group.

On Sundays from March through June and September through November, rangers lead a series of hikes through this scenic park where movies have been filmed since the birth of Hollywood. Even parts of *Jurassic Park* were filmed in its canyons.

Special Outings and Activities

Photography, which older children enjoy as much as adults do, wildflower viewing, and bird watching are all popular activities here. When bird watching, pay attention to the large raptors such as red-tailed hawks and golden eagles that frequently soar overhead.

Star gazing is great at night, and moonlight walks during a full moon are exhilarating.

SADDLEBACK BUTTE STATE PARK
17102 East Avenue J, East
Lancaster, CA 93535
(805) 942-0662

A granite outcropping known as Saddle Butte rises 1,000 feet above the surrounding alluvial bottomlands of Antelope Valley in this park, and Joshua trees grow up to its flanks. During the spring the lands around the butte are covered with a riotous wildflower bloom that brings large numbers of visitors from nearby urban and suburban areas.

Summers are hot enough to keep all but the most intrepid campers away, with highs reaching as much as 115 degrees.

Recommended Ages
Poor for toddlers and preschoolers, Excellent for 6–9 and for 10 and over.

Location
The park is seventeen miles east of Lancaster on Avenue J East.

Camping Facilities
This park has fifty primitive sites that accommodate thirty-foot trailers and motor homes. There are no showers, but there is piped water. The campground is open year-round on a first-come, first-served basis.

Hiking Activities
A short nature trail for the whole family is located near the park headquarters, and it leads you to a vista point where the views are particularly impressive during the peak of the spring wildflower bloom.

A longer trail leads to Saddleback peak, which rises about 1,000 feet above the surrounding flatlands. This hike is best for those ten and over, but some younger kids like to make the trek.

You can explore among the substantial Joshua tree forest that covers much of the park near the campground without worrying about trails, and youngsters like to look for lizards and other reptiles there in the cool of the evening after warm days.

Special Outings and Activities

Wildflower season is the real special time to visit this park. Poppies, lupine, and dozens of other wildflowers bloom in profusion after winter rains have passed, and walks through the fields where the flowers grow provide kids with a close-up of many blossoms they have never seen before.

SAN BERNARDINO NATIONAL FOREST

Forest Supervisor
1824 South Commercenter Circle
San Bernardino, CA 92408-3430
(714) 383-5588

Elevations in this rugged forest range from 1,000 to over 11,000 feet. The Pacific Crest Trail traverses the five ranger districts for almost 150 miles.

Vegetation ranges from chaparral to desert scrub to conifer forests as the elevation increases, and more than 500 miles of hiking trails lead through all of these. This makes hiking and camping possible throughout the year within the forest.

The forest has three wilderness areas completely within its boundaries and two others that are partially within it.

Recommended Ages

Good to Excellent for all ages.

Location

The forest is some 60 miles east of Los Angeles and 100 miles north of San Diego in Riverside and San Bernardino counties.

Camping Facilities

The most popular camping sites in this national forest are in the Arrowhead and Big Bear ranger districts. There many campgrounds are located near Lake Arrowhead, and Big Bear and Baldwin lakes. None of these campgrounds is large and overdeveloped, though. Dogwood Campground near Lake Arrowhead is the largest with ninety-three sites. Most of the others have twenty to fifty sites and provide families with seclusion and only small crowds.

Other popular groups of campgrounds are found in the San Gorgonio and San Jacinto ranger districts. The campgrounds in San Gorgonio are found along State Route 38 as it winds around the north side of the San Gorgonio Wilderness. The majority of the campgrounds in the San Jacinto Ranger District are located along the western boundary of the Mt. San Jacinto State Wilderness Area off State Route 243.

All of these campgrounds are located between 5,000 and 7,500 feet and offer great getaways for families hoping to escape hot Southern California summers.

Hiking Activities

The best hiking trails lead out of the campgrounds near the San Gorgonio and Mt. San Jacinto State wilderness areas. There you can choose short or long outings according to the ages and stamina of your kids.

There are some short trails near the campgrounds around the lakes, but the areas there are more developed, so you have less wilderness hiking.

Special Outings and Activities

The lakes of this national forest provide some of the best fishing in Southern California, and many families focus their camping trips around fishing.

For those who don't like fishing but do like quiet water sports such as swimming, canoeing, and boating, the campgrounds near the lakes are ideal.

ADDITIONAL STATE AND FEDERAL CAMPGROUNDS

ABOUT
THIS SECTION

W hile I have included my favorite family campsites in the main portion of the text, I realize that others will soon develop their own favorites as they travel around California on camping vacations.

You may want to stay closer to home than any of the sites I have included, or you may want to explore places that are off the beaten path. The entries in Section 2 provide you with a comprehensive list of agencies that operate public campgrounds in California. From these you can choose the regions of the state you would like to explore in more depth.

A quick phone call to the agencies in that region will give you access to full information about where the campgrounds are located and what each offers to families.

I have not included county and regional park districts in the list, although some, such as the East Bay Regional Park District near San Francisco, do operate a number of good campgrounds. These districts tend to be in or near large population centers and most campers who reside near those centers are aware the campgrounds are nearby. If you want to camp near unfamiliar population centers you can call the county parks department in the region to see if they have any campgrounds.

CHAPTER · 7

U.S. ARMY CORPS
OF ENGINEERS SITES

U.S. ARMY CORPS OF ENGINEERS
Sacramento District
1325 J Street
Sacramento, CA 95814-2922
(916) 440-2183

The dams constructed by the Corps of Engineers in California were authorized to provide flood protection and irrigation waters for residents of the state. The reservoirs formed behind the dams have created vast recreational areas, however, that attract large number of water lovers, particularly in the summer months.

All twelve of the Corps of Engineer sites in California that have been developed for recreational activities have campgrounds. These are generally full during the warm months when visitors flock to the sites for fishing, boating, swimming, waterskiing, and other water-oriented activities.

They are less crowded from the time the weather cools in the fall until the first warm rays of summer bring the water temperatures up. During this period the campgrounds are lightly used, but families who wish to hike, ride bikes on seldom used trails, birdwatch, or search for wildflowers on the green hillsides in early spring will find plenty to do with few people to bother them.

Several Army Corps of Engineers reservoirs
such as Lake Sonoma offer good camping in
Northern California.

BLACK BUTTE LAKE
Star Route Box 30
Orland, CA 95963
(916) 865-4781

Two campgrounds with over 150 sites.

EASTMAN LAKE
P.O. Box 67
Raymond, CA 93653
(209) 689-3255

Two campgrounds with about 100 sites.

ENGLEBRIGHT LAKE
P.O. Box 6
Smartville, CA 95977
(916) 639-2342

Eighteen boat-in campgrounds, each with two to four sites.

HENSLEY LAKE
P.O. Box 85
Raymond, CA 93653
(209) 673-5151

Two campgrounds with about 100 campsites.

LAKE ISABELLA
4875 Ponderosa Drive
P.O. Box 3810
Lake Isabella, CA 93240
(619) 379-5646

Six campgrounds with over 750 sites.

LAKE KAWEAH
P.O. Box 346
Lemmoncove, CA 93244
(209) 597-2301

One campground with fifty developed sites.

LAKE MENDOCINO
1160 Lake Mendocino Drive
Ukiah, CA 95482
(707) 462-7581

Five campgrounds with over 200 sites.

LAKE SONOMA
3333 Skaggs Springs Road
Geyserville, CA 95441
(707) 433-9483

One campground with 113 sites.

MARTIS CREEK LAKE
P.O. Box 6
Smartville, CA 95977
(916) 639-2342

One campground with twenty-five sites.

NEW HOGAN LAKE
2713 Hogan Dam Road
Valley Springs, CA 95252
(209) 772-1343

One group, one boat-in, and two family campgrounds.

PINE FLAT LAKE
P.O. Box 117
Piedra, CA 93649
(209) 787-2589

Six campgrounds with over 200 sites.

SUCCESS LAKE
P.O. Box 1072
Porterville, CA 93258
(209) 784-0215

One campground with about fifty sites.

CHAPTER · 8

BUREAU OF LAND MANAGEMENT SITES

BUREAU OF LAND MANAGEMENT, CALIFORNIA STATE OFFICE
2800 Cottage Way, E-2807
Sacramento, CA 95825
(916) 978-4754

Few people think of Bureau of Land Management lands when they begin to plan family camping trips. This is unfortunate because some of the prime wild country left in the U.S. is found on these undeveloped parcels. Michael Hodgson recently wrote *America's Secret Recreation Areas* (Foghorn Press), in which he discusses all the Bureau of Land Management lands of the west. California is well represented with uncrowded, scenic destinations where you can camp almost anywhere on the Bureau's land, even if there are no developed campgrounds.

Frequently there are no developed campgrounds, but for families who like to explore areas where few others go Bureau lands offer great opportunities for camping. Many of these are near preserves for rare or endangered species and offer good access to viewing these animals or plants.

Contact the district and resource area offices of the region you would like to explore and ask for their area maps, which are excellent, and for information about the few developed camping sites found on Bureau of Land Management lands. The following entries are organized by districts and resource areas within the districts.

BAKERSFIELD DISTRICT OFFICE, FEDERAL OFFICE BUILDING
Room 311, 800 Truxton Avenue
Bakersfield, CA 93301
(805) 861-4191

Ten campgrounds with over 300 campsites.

Bishop Resource Area
787 North Main, Suite P
Bishop, CA 93514
(619) 872-4881

Caliente Resource Area
4301 Rosedale Highway
Bakersfield, CA 93308
(805) 861-4236

Folsom Resource Area
63 Natoma Street
Folsom, CA 95630
(916) 985-4474

Hollister Resource Area
P.O. Box 365
Hollister, CA 95024
(408) 637-8183

CALIFORNIA DESERT DISTRICT
6221 Box Springs Boulevard
Riverside, CA 92507
(714) 697-5217

Thirteen campgrounds with about 300 campsites.

Barstow Desert Information Center
831 Barstow Road
Barstow, CA 92311
(619) 256-8313

Barstow Resource Area
150 Coolwater Lane
Barstow, CA 92311
(619) 256-3591

El Centro Resource Area
333 South Waterman Avenue
El Centro, CA 92243
(619) 352-5842

Needles Resource Area
101 West Spikes Road
P.O. Box 888
Needles, CA 92363
(619) 326-3896

Palm Springs-South Coast Resource Area
63-500 Gamet Avenue
North Palm Springs, CA 92258
(619) 251-0812

Ridgecrest Resource Area
300 South Richmond Road
Ridgecrest, CA 93555
(619) 375-7125

SUSANVILLE DISTRICT OFFICE
705 Hall Street
Susanville, CA 96103
(916) 257-5381

Two campgrounds with thirty campsites.

Alturas Resource Area
608 West 12th Street
Alturas, CA 96101
(916) 233-4666

Eagle Lake Resource Area
2545 Riverside Drive
Susanville, CA 96130
(916) 257-0456

Surprise Resource Area
602 Cressler Street
Cedarville, CA 96104
(916) 279-6101

UKIAH DISTRICT OFFICE
555 Leslie Street
Ukiah, CA 95482
(707) 462-3873

Fourteen campgrounds with over 125 sites.

The whole family can splash in the shallow waters of California's rivers on hot summer days.

Arcata Resource Area
1125 16th Street, Room 219
P.O. Box 1112
Arcata, CA 95521
(707) 822-7648

Clear Lake Resource Area
555 Leslie Street
Ukiah, CA 95482
(707) 462-3873

Redding Resource Area
355 Hemsted Drive
Redding, CA 96002
(916) 246-5325

CHAPTER 9

CALIFORNIA STATE FORESTS

W hile national forests include some of the prime recreational destinations in California, and the campgrounds found in them frequently are as good if not better than those found in state and national parks, state forests have been only slightly developed for recreation. They are primarily research forests set aside for demonstration purposes.

Nevertheless, each of the four state forests offers some excellent camping. The facilities are generally rustic to undeveloped, but their setting and lack of crowds more than offset their lack of development. If you want to explore the natural world of California forests, want at least minimal campground development, and don't want to battle crowds for campsites, then state forests may be where you will want to head.

BOGGS MOUNTAIN STATE FOREST
P.O. Box 839
Cobb, CA 95426
(707) 928-4378

Three primitive campgrounds with twenty sites. This forest is near Clear Lake and a highly developed tourist area, but there is little spillover into the forest campgrounds from the thousands who descend on the lake on summer weekends.

JACKSON STATE FOREST
802 North Main Street
P.O. Box 1185
Fort Bragg, CA 95437
(707) 964-5674

Twenty-two campgrounds with from one to sixteen sites. This site is just inland from some of the most popular beaches and state parks along the North Coast. The roads through the forest are primitive dirt roads, but the forests are great examples of mixed, second-growth fir and redwood, and the beaches are within an easy drive if you want to take day trips.

Also, along the western edge of the forest are examples of

A banana slug searches for food on a redwood log.

the unique "pygmy forests" that struggle to survive on the inhospitable lands along the stair-stepped marine terraces that rise from the Mendocino Coast.

LATOUR STATE FOREST
1000 Cypress Avenue
Redding, CA 96001
(916) 225-2445

There are four designated campgrounds with about a dozen sites here. This forest is part of the Cascade Range to the east of Redding, and supports ten species of coniferous trees that have commercial value.

MOUNTAIN HOME STATE FOREST
P.O. Box 517
Springville, CA 93265
(209) 539-2855 (winter)
(209) 539-2321 (summer)

Mountain Home has seven campgrounds with almost 100 undeveloped sites. Balch County Park, with 80 sites, is within forest boundaries. This forest is located 5,000–7,000 feet in elevation in the southern Sierra Nevada within the Sequoia National Forest.

CHAPTER 10

CALIFORNIA STATE PARKS

CALIFORNIA DEPARTMENT OF PARKS AND RECREATION
P.O. Box 942896
Sacramento, CA 94296
(916) 653-6995

alifornia has one of the best state park systems in the country, and campers flock to popular parks year-round. You can find uncrowded parks many times of the year, though, and campgrounds are laid out so that even during the busy seasons most individual campsites provide a modicum of privacy.

If you wish to head for a park that is likely to be crowded, make reservations up to eight weeks in advance of your planned arrival date. At the most popular state parks you should make reservations early if you want to arrive on a Friday or a Saturday. It is usually easier to get campsites if you begin your stay on a Tuesday or Wednesday. Call (800) 444-PARK for state park campground reservations.

The park system provides campsites for car campers, walk-in campers, backpackers, and horse campers. Fourteen parks even provide horses and related equipment for a fee. Most others have picnic tables, barbecue stoves or fireplaces, and pit toilets for equestrian campers. Equestrians can also make reservations for the campsites by calling (800) 444-PARK.

The park system is divided into six regions (I have followed these divisions in Section 1), and the units in each division offer widely different activities and surroundings. All the state park units that provide camping are listed below, along with the principal features of the parks.

NORTH COAST

Austin Creek State Recreation Area
(707) 869-2015

The 4,200 acres of grassy hillsides, oak woodlands, and scattered pines in the recreation area offer a sharp contrast to the neighboring Armstrong Grove Redwood Preserve. Twenty-four campsites. Near Guerneville, off State Route 116. (See full description in Section 1, page 21.)

Benbow Lake State Recreation Area
(707) 946-2311

This tiny reservoir on the south fork of the Eel River is dammed up for each summer season and is ideal for canoeists and paddleboaters. Park rangers lead canoe "hikes" during summer. The park, home of summer Shakespeare and art festivals, features seventy-six campsites and is located two miles south of Garberville off U.S. 101.

Del Norte Coast Redwoods State Park
(707) 464-9533

Combine spectacular Pacific coastline with dense stands of old-growth redwoods and you have a great family outing. Roosevelt elk and other redwood forest dwellers are seen regularly in the park, which is located about seven miles south of Crescent City on U.S. 101. The park has 145 campsites. (See full description in Section 1, page 23.)

Fort Ross State Historic Park
(707) 847-3286

This fort marks Russia's southern-most permanent California outpost. The 1,160-acre park is twelve miles north of Jenner on State Route 1. Reef Campground, with twenty-five sites is ten miles to north.

Grizzly Creek Redwoods State Park
(707) 777-3683 or 946-2311

Northeast of Garberville, this is one of California's smallest and least-visited redwood state parks. The 390-acre park has thirty campsites and is located on State Route 36, about eighteen miles east of U.S. 101. State Route 36 is steep when approaching the park from the east, so vehicles pulling trailers should avoid it. (See full description in Section 1, page 28.)

Hendy Woods State Park
(707) 937-5804

This park is famous for the fallen redwood stump that was home for a man known locally as the Boonville Hermit. It is located eight miles northwest of Boonville, a half mile south of State Route 128 on Philo-Greenwood Road. It has ninety-two sites. (See full description in Section 1, page 30.)

Humboldt Lagoons State Park and
Harry A. Merlo State Recreation Area
(707) 488-2171

There are three lagoons within the two parks. During heavy storms, Stone Lagoon and Big Lagoon can overflow, with the exit stream carving a deep channel. Their water levels can then drop by as much as six feet an hour. Later the surf and tide repair the beach. It is thirty-two miles north of Eureka on U.S. 101, and features twenty sites.

Humboldt Redwoods State Park
(707) 946-2409

Exit U.S. 101 at Humboldt Redwoods State Park and take the thirty-three-mile-long Avenue of the Giants. It travels through 51,143 acres of the most impressive stands of California's old growth redwoods. Within Humboldt lies the 10,000-acre Rockefeller Forest, which preserves nearly one-eighth of the old-growth redwoods remaining in the world. The park has 247 sites. (See full description in Section 1, page 31.)

Jedediah Smith Redwoods State Park
(707) 458-3310 or 464-9533

A beautiful redwood grove covers more than 5,000 acres of this 9,500-acre park. The park has 108 sites, miles of hiking trails, and one of the state's largest redwood trees, located on State Route 199, nine miles northeast of Crescent City. (See full description in Section 1, page 34.)

MacKerricher State Park
(707) 937-5804

Eight miles of beach offers refuge for harbor seals and a playground for hikers, bicyclists, and fishermen, along with wheelchair access to the more popular areas of the 1,600-acre park. From November through March the park's headland offers a great vantage point for viewing migrating whales. The park has 143 sites and is three miles north of Fort Bragg on State Route 1, near the town of Cleone. (See full description in Section 1, page 36.)

Manchester State Beach
(707) 937-5804

The San Andreas Fault runs into the ocean at 1,400-acre Manchester State Beach in southern Mendocino County. The park offers winter steelhead running in two creeks, habitat for whistling swans, great surf fishing, five miles of sandy beach, and forty-eight sites. The entrance is a half mile north of the town of Manchester on State Route 1.

Patrick's Point State Park
(707) 677-3570

Whale-watching, wandering miles of beach, exploring tide

pools, and searching for agates are popular family activities at Patrick's Point. Sumeg, a recently constructed Yurok Indian village, is a popular new addition to the park, which is located a half mile west of U.S. 101, five miles north of Trinidad. It has 123 sites. (See full description in Section 1, page 38.)

Prairie Creek Redwoods State Park
(707) 488-2171

Paralleling eight miles of U.S. 101, fifty miles north of Eureka, lies one of California's most popular redwood parks. Roosevelt elk graze in the open prairie adjacent to the highway and along much of Gold Bluffs Beach. Fern Canyon, a steep-sided canyon whose walls are blanketed with ferns, is just one of dozens of hiking destinations in the 12,544-acre park. There are 100 campsites. (See full description in Section 1, page 44.)

Richardson Grove State Park
(707) 247-3318 or 946-2311

Many families have been visiting "The Grove" each year for generations. The south fork of the Eel River slices through the park, where swimmers enjoy the cool waters in the summer. The park, with 169 sites, is located eight miles south of Garberville on U.S. 101. (See full description in Section 1, page 46.)

Russian Gulch State Park
(707) 937-5804

The ocean is only a small, but popular, part of this 1,300-acre park. Ocean waves, entering the "Punch Bowl" through a tunnel, churn inside a large, collapsed sea cave, giving the appearance of a boiling cauldron. Inland, there is a 36-foot-high waterfall, miles of hiking trails, and a paved bicycle trail. The park also has thirty sites and a primitive horse camp. The park is off State Route 1 just north of Mendocino.

Salt Point State Park
(707) 847-3221 or 865-2391

This 6,000-acre park includes six miles of rugged North Coast along with inland mountains reaching 1,000 feet above sea level. Many miles of hiking and horseback riding trails are found in the park, with one trail leading to the intriguing Pygmy Forest. Dozens of beautiful sandy coves are hidden along the shoreline. The park, 130 sites, is located twenty miles north of Jenner on State Route 1. (See full description in Section 1, page 48.)

Sinkyone Wilderness State Park
(707) 986-7711

This rugged land of forests, prairies, bluffs, and beaches has limited access over steep, winding gravel roads. Hikers and backpackers visit here to walk the fifteen-mile trail that stretches the length of the park. A permit is needed for overnight backpacking stays in its primitive sites. South end access is via County Road 431, which leaves State Route 1 at milepost 90.88 between Leggett and the coast. (See full description in Section 1, page 53.)

Sonoma Coast State Beach
(707) 875-3483

More than ten miles of coastline with steep cliffs, long sandy beaches, and constantly shifting dunes lie within the park's 5,000 acres. Bodega Head, to the south, is known for winter whale watching, and there is a large seal rookery near the mouth of the Russian River. There are 128 sites. The state beach stretches between Jenner and Bodega Bay on State Route 1. (See full description in Section 1, page 60.)

Standish-Hickey State Recreation Area
(707) 925-6482 or 946-2311

Few North Coast travelers head for this 1,020-acre redwood park that lies about one mile north of Leggett adjacent to U.S. 101. Those who do seldom find crowds fishing and swimming in the south fork of the Eel River, which bisects the park. Nine miles of trails lead to small redwood groves. There are

162 campsites. (See full description in Section 1, page 63.)

Sugarloaf Ridge State Park
(707) 833-5712 or 938-1519

Twenty-five miles crisscross the 2,700 acres at Sugarloaf Ridge that range in elevation from 600 to 2,729 feet at the summit of Bald Mountain. On clear days you can view the Sierra Nevada and the Golden Gate from the peaks. The park is north of State Route 12 on Adobe Canyon Road, seven miles east of Santa Rosa. It has fifty sites. (See full description in Section 1, page 65.)

Van Damme State Park
(707) 937-5804

Abalone divers enjoy the park's sheltered and easily reached beach, but it is the ten miles of trails that follow the Little River through much of the 2,160-acre park that attracts many visitors. At the top of the ridge above the park is a pygmy forest where fir and redwood trees reach only a tenth of their normal height. The park is located three miles south of Mendocino on State Route 1, and features seventy-four sites. (See full description in Section 1, page 67.)

Westport-Union Landing State Beach
(707) 937-5804

This park, used mostly by locals, is two miles north of Westport off State Route 1. The forty-one-acre park is a narrow two-mile-long strip. Its primitive campground sits on coastal bluffs above the crashing ocean waves and is a haven for tide pool explorers, surf fishermen, abalone divers, and spear fishing enthusiasts.

NORTH INLAND

Ahjumawi Lava Springs State Park
(916) 335-2777

An underground river that drains Tule Lake more than fifty

miles away surfaces near this park northeast of Redding. Canoeists and boaters explore the 6,000-acre park's waterways, spring-fed pools, and lava flows. The only access is by boats launched on Main Street in the town of McArthur. Only primitive camping is available.

Auburn State Recreation Area
(916) 885-4527

Recreationists flock to this park's 42,000 acres even though construction on the controversial Auburn Dam has been stalled for several decades. The north and middle forks of the American River offer fifty miles of white water, steep canyons, and oak and pine woodlands. There is limited vehicular access to Lake Clementine where there is fishing, boating, and 100 campsites. The park office is located on State Route 49, one mile south of Auburn.

Bothe-Napa Valley State Park
(707) 942-4575

This 1,917-acre state park has several trails, a swimming pool, and fifty developed campsites. The park is located four miles north of St. Helena on State Route 29. (See full description in Section 1, page 73.)

Castle Crags State Park
(916) 235-2684 or 225-2065

The crags in this park are a landmark to travelers along I-5. The 4,000-acre park lies at the base of the granite spires that tower more that 4,000 feet above the nearby upper reaches of the Sacramento River. The park is located six miles south of Dunsmuir and has sixty-four sites. (See full description in Section 1, page 76.)

Clear Lake State Park
(707) 279-4293

This park is on the south end of California's second largest freshwater lake, which offers excellent fishing most of the year. Summer brings swimmers and water-skiers to the lake's relatively warm waters. The park has 147 sites. The entrance is 3.5 miles northeast of Kelseyville on Soda Bay Road.

Colusa-Sacramento River State Recreation Area
(916) 458-4927

The land along the river here belonged to the River Patwin long before 1872, when John Muir camped near what is now the park. People still head for the region and enjoy the park's sixty-seven acres of campsites (twenty-two sites), picnic sites, and a launch ramp for small boats. The park is near downtown Colusa, nine miles east of I-5 on State Route 20, north of Sacramento. (See full description in Section 1, page 78.)

D.L. Bliss State Park
(916) 525-7277

One of Lake Tahoe's finest beaches is found at this park, but get there early on summer days because the small beach parking lot fills quickly. Several trails, one along the lake shore

Kids like to strike out on their own during day hikes.

and another to Balancing Rock, lead away from the crowded beach. The park is located seventeen miles south of Tahoe City on State Route 89, and just a couple of miles north of Emerald Bay. The state park has 168 sites. (See full description in Section 1, page 80.)

Donner Memorial State Park
(916) 587-3841

The winter of 1846–1847 proved to be one of the most severe ever to hit the Sierra, and it unfortunately coincided with the Donner Party's attempted crossing of the precipitous mountains. Many members of party died of starvation or froze to death in the blizzards that struck the 7,200-foot mountain pass. The park sits on 353 acres near where the Donner Party spent the winter and offers swimming, camping (154 sites), picnic sites, and the Emigrant Trail Museum. The park is west of Truckee off I-80. (See full description in Section 1, page 82.)

Emerald Bay State Park
(916) 541-3030

Adjacent to D.L. Bliss State Park is Emerald Bay, one of Lake Tahoe's most photographed natural attractions. Vikingsholm, a replica of a Scandinavian medieval castle, is part of the state park that surrounds the bay. A one-mile hike leads down to the castle where tours are offered during summer. The park is twenty-two miles south of Tahoe City on State Route 89 and has 100 campsites. (See full description in Section 1, page 87.)

Folsom Lake State Recreation Area
(916) 988-0205

The 18,000-acre Folsom Lake sits in the Sierra foothills gold country, offering welcome relief from the hot summers of the Sacramento Valley. Activities include fishing, swimming, boating, bicycling, jogging, and hiking. The park can be reached by crossing the American River to the town of Folsom and driving north on Folsom-Auburn Road. It has 180 campsites. (See full description in Section 1, page 88.)

Grover Hot Springs State Park
(916) 694-2248 or 525-7232

Hot mineral springs that reach 102 degrees draw families to this High Sierra park where the surrounding mountain peaks intercept most of the snow that would otherwise fall on Grover Hot Springs during the winter. Enough snow still accumulates for excellent cross-country skiing, and during winter seventeen of seventy-four campsites usually remain open. Most people prefer to head for the park during the mild summers, though. Grover Hot Springs State Park is located south of Lake Tahoe, three miles west of Markleeville on Hot Springs Road.

Lake Oroville State Recreation Area
(916) 538-2200

In years of high water, the lake boasts 167 miles of shoreline and 23 square miles of surface. The water from Feather Falls, one of North America's highest waterfalls, drops 640 feet before it enters an arm of the lake. Activities near the campgrounds include fishing, camping (299 sites), swimming, hiking, and water-skiing. Lake Oroville is located seven miles east of Oroville on State Route 162.

Malakoff Diggins State Historic Park
(916) 265-2740

The decimation of whole mountains by hydraulic mining in the last century is still evident in the hills of this 2,700-acre historic park. Legal battles between mine owners and downstream farmers and communities ended the gold mining technique of washing away entire mountains using powerful streams of water. The park and the town of North Bloomfield are about sixteen miles northeast of Nevada City on North Bloomfield Road, which is graveled and steep. The park features thirty sites. (See full description in Section 1, page 99.)

McArthur-Burney Falls Memorial State Park
(916) 335-2777 or 335-5483

Perhaps more impressive than the 129-foot-high waterfall is the fact that 100 million gallons of water flow over the falls each day. Additional water emerges from springs across the face of the falls, which joins to create a mist-filled basin of lush green vegetation. The park is northeast of Redding, six miles north of State Route 299, on State Route 89 near Burney. There are 128 sites. (See full description in Section 1, page 102.)

Plumas Eureka State Park
(916) 836-2380

Mining began here north of Lake Tahoe in the 1850s and continued until World War II. The 6,700-acre park protects the remains of the Mohawk Stamp Mill and several other buildings. You can camp at its sixty-seven campsites and also fish in its streams and lakes during summer. In winter there is cross-country and downhill skiing. The park's museum and visitor center are located five miles west of Blairsden on County Road A14. (See full description in Section 1, page 109.)

Sugar Pine Point State Park
(916) 525-7982

The largest of the Tahoe area state parks is also the only state park in the lake basin that keeps its campground open year-round. Summer brings hoards of campers who stay at its 175 campsites and who love the beach areas of the park or want to tour the Ehrman Mansion. Winter brings hearty campers who come to explore several miles of cross-country ski trails. The 2,011-acre park is ten miles south of Tahoe City on State Route 89. (See full description in Section 1, page 117.)

Tahoe State Recreation Area
(916) 583-3074 or 525-7982

On the edge of Tahoe City is a small campground near a shopping center with shops, restaurants, and a grocery store. This thirteen-acre park offers excellent views of Lake Tahoe and direct access to the lake shoreline and a pier. The park is closed in winter. Tahoe State Recreation Area is on State Route 28, near the east end of Tahoe City. It has thirty-nine campsites.

Woodson Bridge State Recreation Area
(916) 839-2112

The 428 acres of meadows that flank the banks of the Sacramento River in this park attract hoards of fishing enthusiasts who come for the annual runs of shad, steelhead, striped bass, and salmon. Families also come to explore the wild areas of the riparian forest and swim in the backwaters of the river. The west bank remains relatively undeveloped with only a boat-in campsite, while the east shore features a campground. The park has forty-six campsites and is located northwest of Chico, adjacent to Tehama County Park, on South Avenue, six miles east of Corning between I-5 and State Route 99.

CENTRAL COAST

Andrew Molera State Park
(408) 667-2315

This large state park's 4,800 mostly undeveloped acres receive relatively light use. The Big Sur River meanders through the park on its way to the Pacific, and miles of trails wind through meadows, along beaches, over hilltops, and to walk-in primitive campsites. Hikers and bicyclists use the popular primitive trail camp, located about one-third of a mile from the parking area. The park is located twenty miles south of Carmel on State Route 1.

Big Basin Redwoods State Park
(408) 338-6132

Big Basin is California's oldest state park, established early in this century. The park has grown to over 18,000 acres, with many miles of trails that pass streams, waterfalls, and giant redwoods. There are six trail camps, thirty-six tent cabins, a store, and a gift shop in addition to the developed camp-grounds. In all there are more than 188 campsites. The park is located twenty miles north of Santa Cruz via State Routes 9 and 236. (See full description in Section 1, page 125.)

Butano State Park
(415) 879-0173

This 3,200-acre park is located in the Santa Cruz Mountains, only three miles from the ocean. Trails, many open to bicy-clists, meander through coastal scrub and redwood forests. The high mountains afford views of Ano Nuevo Island. The park has twenty-one developed campsites and is located five miles south of Pescadero on Cloverdale Road or from Gazos Creek Road off State Route 1. (See full description in Section 1, page 127.)

China Camp State Park
(415) 456-0766

This 620-acre park preserves the site of San Francisco Bay's last Chinese shrimp fishing village that thrived here in the 1880s. Most people come for the day to watch the bird life or to hike, swim, fish, boat, or windsurf. Others come to enjoy an overnight or more in the walk-in campground (thirty-one sites). China Camp is located on North San Pedro Road, four miles east of San Rafael and U.S. 101.

Fremont Peak State Park
(408) 623-4255 or 623-4526

At 3,169 feet in elevation, this mountain offers vistas of San Benito Valley and Monterey Bay. Visitors can enjoy primitive camping, several group camps, an equestrian camp, picnic facilities, and an astronomical observatory. There are twenty-five campsites. Trailers are not recommended. Take San Juan Canyon Road and follow the signs for eleven miles south from San Juan Bautista and State Route 156.

Gaviota State Park
(805) 968-1711

Gaviota Peak, which rises 2,458 feet above the ocean in this 2,700-acre park, offers a spectacular view of the Channel Islands. U.S. 101 bisects the park, which is located thirty-three miles west of Santa Barbara. There are fifty-nine campsites.

Henry Cowell Redwoods State Park
(408) 335-9145

The redwoods of Henry Cowell Park grow at a lower elevation, with a slightly drier climate, than those of nearby Big Basin Redwoods State Park. The park features a nature center, gift shop, and riding and hiking trails, and 113 campsites. It is located near Felton on State Route 9, in the Santa Cruz Mountains. (See full description in Section 1, page 129.)

Hollister Hills State Vehicle Recreation Area
(408) 637-3874

This off-road park attracts motorcyclists and four-wheel-drive buffs who enjoy its 140 miles of trails and 125 campsites. Call ahead to make sure a special event is not scheduled. It is located about six miles south of Hollister on Cienega Road.

Montana de Oro State Park
(805) 772-2560 or 528-0513

South of Morro Bay are the 8,000 acres of Montana de Oro, with 3.5 miles of coastline. A rugged network of cliffs, hidden coves, and small, sandy beaches combines to make this a great place to explore the ocean shore. The best beach is at Spooners Cove. The park entrance is seven miles south of Los Osos on Pecho Road. There are fifty sites.

Morro Bay State Park
(805) 772-2560

Morro Bay State Park offers boating, fishing, bird watching, and golfing on an eighteen-hole public course. It also has 135 campsites. Perched on cliffs overlooking the bay is the

Museum of Natural History. It houses displays that explain the area's complex ecosystem. The park is located in the small community of Morro Bay, just off State Route 1. (See full description in Section 1, page 133.)

Morro Strand State Beach
(805) 772-2560

A three-mile stretch of sandy beach connects the northern and southern entrances of Morro Strand State Beach. Take the Yerba Buena exit, a short distance north of town. Three miles north of Morro Bay, 24th Street allows access to the northern part of the state beach. There are 104 campsites. (See full description in Section 1, page 134.)

Mount Tamalpais State Park
(415) 388-2070

This 6,300-acre park just north of San Francisco is primarily for day use. Ten rustic cabins perched on a bluff overlooking the Pacific are popular for those who want to enjoy a rustic outing overlooking the ocean. The park is a hiker's paradise, with sixteen campsites, and the twisting road to the top of the 2,571-foot summit attracts bicyclists. Most people, however, drive to the top. The park is located off State Route 1 between Mill Valley and Stinson Beach.

Pajaro Coast State Park and State Beaches
(408) 688-3241

Along State Route 1, from just north of Santa Cruz to south near Moss Landing, several state beaches and one state park offer access to the coastline. In Santa Cruz, Natural Bridges State Beach is famous for the monarch butterflies that migrate to its eucalyptus grove each fall.

In summer, swimmers and surfers congregate at New Brighton State Beach, Seacliff State Beach, Manresa State Beach, Sunset State Beach, and Twin Lakes State Beach. New Brighton, Seacliff, and Sunset state beaches also offer campgrounds. Another main attraction is a trail system used by equestrians and bicyclists. All told, there are 231 campsites.

Pfeiffer-Big Sur State Park
(408) 667-2315

Big Sur is a spectacular state park of 821 acres of redwoods, conifers, oaks, and open meadows. For some reason, the redwoods here do not gain the height of their northern cousins. The park is located twenty-six miles south of Carmel on State Route 1. There are 217 sites. (See full description on page 136.)

Pismo State Beach
(805) 489-2684

Six miles of wide, sandy beach here backed by dunes that have been the scene of many Hollywood movies. Some people come to go clamming for Pismo clams. There are two campgrounds in the 1,000-acre park, one of which offers RV hookups, and 185 sites. The park is located two miles south of the town of Pismo Beach off State Route 1.

Portola State Park
(415) 948-9098

South and east of Half Moon Bay, this 2,400-acre state park is covered by Douglas fir, oaks, and giant coast redwoods. City dwellers come here for a quiet break from the rigors of daily life. The park has fifteen miles of hiking trails, fifty-two campsites, and at 300 feet in height, one of the tallest redwoods in Santa Cruz County. It is located six miles off State Route 35. (See full description in Section 1, page 140.)

Samuel P. Taylor State Park
(415) 488-9897

Within Samuel P. Taylor State Park's 2,700 acres lie open hillsides laced with hiking and equestrian trails, rushing creeks, and cool canyons where redwoods thrive. Steelhead and salmon still enter Papermill Creek in the park, but fishing is not permitted because of a major decline in the fish population during the past several years. The park has sixty camp-sites. It is located fifteen miles west of San Rafael on Sir Francis Drake Boulevard. (See full description on page 51.)

San Simeon State Park
(805) 927-2020

For those wishing to tour nearby Hearst Castle, the park offers the nearest camping. The campground is open all year (213 sites), and campers enjoy the two miles of coastline that also includes three day-use areas between Cambria and San Simeon. The coast access areas draw beachcombers, ocean shore fishing enthusiasts, and sunset watchers. The state beach is located north of San Luis Obispo, about five miles south of Hearst Castle on State Route 1.

CENTRAL INLAND

Brannan Island State Recreation Area
(916) 777-6671

Northeast of San Francisco Bay, a maze of waterways web the Sacramento–San Joaquin Delta creating an almost end-less adventure for boaters and fishermen. Islands and marshes throughout the region offer prime wildlife habitat and excellent fishing opportunities. Brannan Island State Recreation Area has a boat launch, picnic facilities, and 100 campsites. The park is located along State Route 160, three miles south of Rio Vista. (See full description on page 75.)

Calaveras Big Trees State Park
(209) 795-2334

Among the largest living things in the world are the giant sequoias found in Calaveras Big Trees State Park located northeast of Stockton. Two groves of big trees, now protected, survived heavy nineteenth-century logging. The park is located four miles northeast of Arnold on State Route 4 and has 129 sites. (See full description in Section 1, page 148.)

Swirling water holds a fascination for all ages.

Caswell Memorial State Park
(209) 599-3810

As the Stanislaus River slows through the San Joaquin Valley, great stands of riparian oak forests are created. About 258 acres of oaks, willows, and cottonwood trees provide homes for an abundance of wildlife, including a protected nesting site of great blue herons. You can spend a quiet day here fishing or swimming. The park is located on Austin Road, five miles off State Route 99, south of Manteca, and has sixty-five sites. (See full description on page 145.)

Colonel Allensworth State Historic Park
(805) 849-3433

In 1908, a group of Black Americans, led by Colonel Allen Allensworth, established a small farming community in the San Joaquin Valley. Uncontrollable circumstances, including a drop in the area's water table, resulted in the demise of the town. Today, with a continuing restoration program and special events, the town is coming back to life as a state historic park. Allensworth is located north of Bakersfield, seven miles west of Earlimart and State Route 99 on County Road J22. It has fifteen campsites.

George J. Hatfield State Recreation Area
(209) 632-1852

Near the confluence of the San Joaquin and Merced rivers, this forty-six-acre park contains oak woodlands and lawn areas. Activities include swimming, fishing, and camping at its twenty-one sites. From I-5, take the Newman exit and drive east for five miles on County Road J18 to the park entrance, which is just past the San Joaquin River bridge.

Henry W. Coe State Park
(408) 779-2728

A 125-mile trail system laces the park's 68,000 acres of canyons, oak woodlands, and pine covered hillsides. Summer fire hazards often require restrictions of activities. The park is located about forty minutes from Morgan Hill and U.S. 101 via Dunne Avenue. There are twenty-one sites here. (See full description in Section 1, page 154.)

Indian Grinding Rock State Historic Park
(209) 296-7488

The park offers camping year-round among the pines and oak woodlands where Miwoks once lived. The Chaw'se Regional Indian Museum offers visitors an excellent introduction to the Miwok way of life. Outside, a village has been constructed that is used today for various celebrations and ceremonies by numerous California Native American communities. The park, with twenty-one campsites, is northeast of Stockton, about one mile up Pine Grove-Volcano Road from State Route 88 between Jackson and Pine Grove. (See full description in Section 1, page 155.)

McConnell State Recreation Area
(209) 394-7755

After cascading its way from Yosemite Valley, the Merced River slows its march to the ocean as it passes through McConnell State Recreation Area. This small park provides an abundance of picnicking, camping (sixteen sites), swimming, and fishing facilities. The State Recreation Area is located southeast of the town of Delhi on State Route 99, south of Turlock.

Millerton Lake State Recreation Area
(209) 822-2225 or 822-2332

In 1944, the San Joaquin River was dammed, creating Millerton Lake. An old county courthouse, built in 1867, was moved above the rising waters and is now part of the 6,500-acre park. In the summer, families come to swim, fish, and participate in water sports such as boating and waterskiing. In the winter birders come to view the large colony of bald eagles that winters here. The recreation area is located twenty miles northeast of Fresno via State Routes 41 and 145. There are 131 sites.

Mount Diablo State Park
(415) 837-2525

More than 40,000 square miles of California are visible from the summit of 3,849-foot Mount Diablo. On a clear day, you can see Mount Lassen, Mount Whitney, and the Sierra Nevada. The park is on Diablo Road, five miles east of I-680 from Danville. It can also be reached from Walnut Creek via Ygnacio Valley Road. The park has sixty sites. (See full description in Section 1, page 162.)

San Luis Reservoir State Recreation Area
(209) 826-1196

San Luis Reservoir is part of the California Aqueduct system. The reservoir is composed of three artificial lakes that provide fishing, water-skiing, swimming, and windsurfing. Boaters should be aware of the sudden high winds that can develop. The park is located on State Route 152, twelve miles west of Los Banos. The park has seventy-nine sites.

Turlock Lake State Recreation Area
(209) 874-2008

The Tuolumne River originates high in the Sierra and tumbles down to Turlock Lake in the foothills above the San Joaquin Valley west of Yosemite. The reservoir offers boating, waterskiing, swimming, and picnicking. The Tuolumne River also offers visitors swimming, fishing, and canoeing. The Lake Road turnoff to Turlock Lake is located about twenty miles east of Modesto on State Route 132. There are sixty-five campsites.

SOUTH COAST

Carpinteria State Beach
(805) 684-2811 or 654-4611

The Spanish named this area Carpinteria because they found that the Chumash tribe had a large, oceangoing canoe-building enterprise, or "carpentry shop" located here. The Chumash chose the spot because of the naturally occurring surface tar they used to seal their boats. The park offers a mile of great swimming beach, tide pools, and 174 sites. The park can be reached via State Route 224, off U.S. 101, twelve miles south of Santa Barbara.

Doheny State Beach
(714) 496-6171 or 492-0802

This relatively small park is one of southern California's better camping spots. The sixty-two-acre parcel has a mile of sandy beach, while its rocky north end attracts tide pool explorers and anglers. The entrance is on Del Obispo Street off Pacific Coast Highway at Dana Point. There are 162 sites.

El Capitan State Beach
(805) 968-1711

One of three popular parks north of Santa Barbara, El Capitan offers rocky tide pools, a sandy beach, and stands of sycamore and oak providing a beautiful setting for swimming, fishing, or surfing. A stairway gives access to the beach area from the bluffs above. A bike trail connects with Refugio State Beach, about 2.5 miles away. El Capitan is located off U.S. 101, seventeen miles west of Santa Barbara. There are 140 campsites.

Leo Carrillo State Beach
(818) 880-0350

This state beach, named after a 1950s radio and television celebrity, has 1.5 miles of beach used by swimmers, surfers, windsurfers, and beachcombers. Giant sycamores shade two campgrounds, with 138 sites. The park is located in the Santa Monica Mountains, twenty-five miles northwest of Santa Monica on the Pacific Coast Highway. (See full description in Section 1, page 186.)

Malibu Creek State Park
(818) 880-0350

This 6,600-acre park was once used by Twentieth Century Fox for shooting numerous movie and TV productions including *M.A.S.H.* and *Planet of the Apes.* The park is set in the rugged Santa Monica Mountains and offers miles of trails for hikers, equestrians, and mountain bikers. Families can fish in a creek and small lake. The park is located off Las Virgenes Road, four miles south of U.S. 101. There are sixty campsites.

Point Mugu State Park
(818) 880-0350

The 14,980-acre park includes the jagged pinnacles of the Boney Mountain State Wilderness Area, open meadows, canyons filled with oaks and sycamores, and a beach area. Miles of equestrian, biking, and hiking trails traverse the park. It is located in the Santa Monica Mountains, thirty-one miles west of Santa Monica, off the Pacific Coast Highway. There are 150 campsites. (See full description in Section 1, page 187.)

Refugio State Beach
(805) 968-1711

Palm trees have been planted near Refugio Creek to lend a tropical look to this beach and camping area. There are plenty of picnic areas at the 1.5-mile beach. A bike trail along the bluff ties Refugio with nearby El Capitan State Beach, 2.5 miles east. The park is located off U.S. 101, twenty-three miles northwest of Santa Barbara. There are eighty-five campsites.

San Clemente State Beach
(714) 492-3156 or 492-0802

San Clemente is a camping park along one of the most scenic stretches of California coast. It has 157 campsites. Trails lead to a mile of beach that is popular with surfers, body surfers, swimmers, and divers. The park entrance is reached via the Avenida Calafia exit off I-5 near the south end of San Clemente.

San Diego Coast State Parks and State Beaches
(619) 729-8947

Along California's southern-most coast, from the Mexican border north to Carlsbad, are miles of beautiful beaches. Carlsbad State Beach, South Carlsbad State Beach, Leucadia State Beach, San Elijo State Beach, and Cardiff State Beach all lie north of San Diego, west of I-5. Silver Strand State Beach and Border Field State Park are south of San Diego. All together there are 397 sites. (See full description on page 189.)

San Onofre State Beach
(714) 492-4872 or 492-0802

The 3,000-acre park's 221-site campground has been developed along the abandoned portion of the coast highway. The campground is situated on sandstone bluffs overlooking 3.5 miles of beach that beckons swimmers, surfers, and sunbathers. The park entrance is located three miles down Basilone Road, off I-5, near the San Diego and Orange county line.

Santa Monica Area State Beaches
(213) 456-8432 or (818) 706-1310 for state-run beaches
(800) 533-PARK for beaches operated by Los Angeles county

Miles of beautiful Southern California public beaches are found along the Pacific Coast Highway near Santa Monica. They include Malibu Lagoon State Beach, Las Tunas State Beach, Santa Monica State Beach, Dockweiler State Beach, Manhattan State Beach, Redondo State Beach, Point Dume State Beach, and Robert H. Meyer Memorial State Beach. Some are operated by Los Angeles County and others by the California Department of Parks and Recreation. All offer excellent swimming, sunbathing, and surfing opportunities.

Ventura Area State Beaches
(805) 654-3951 for Ventura County beaches
(805) 654-4611 for state-run beaches

Near the coastal towns of Ventura and Oxnard lie three state beaches, Emma Wood, San Buenaventura, and McGrath. All offer swimming, surfing, and fishing. San Buenaventura State Beach features a 1,700-foot-long pier. There are 235 sites.

SOUTH INLAND

Anza-Borrego Desert State Park
(619) 767-5311

Anza-Borrego became California's first desert state park in 1933. Since then it has also become the state's largest, protecting more than 600,000 acres of Colorado Desert. Eroded badlands sprawl at near sea level elevation, and pinon–juniper woodlands cover 6,000-foot mountains. Located east of San Diego, the park is reached via State Routes 78 and 79 from the east and by I-8 from the south. There are 142 developed sites and unlimited primitive camping sites. (See full description in Section 1, page 195)

Cuyamaca Rancho State Park
(619) 765-0755

Set in the Peninsular Range, Cuyamaca Rancho is one of Southern California's largest parks, spreading over 24,677 acres of open meadows, forested mountains, and oak woodlands. The park is popular with San Diego families who come here to escape the city. Winters are relatively cold for Southern California and sometimes snowy. The park has excellent facilities, trails for equestrians and hikers, and 182 campsites. It is located nine miles north of I-8 on State Route 79. (See full description in Section 1, page 199.)

Lake Elsinore State Recreation Area
(714) 657-0676 or 674-3005

The lake, set at the base of the steep eastern side of the Santa Ana Mountains, has been a resort since the 1880s. A concessionaire operates a boat launching ramp, a campground with 500 sites, and a picnic area. Fishing and waterskiing are the lake's main activities. Lake Elsinore is located on State Route 74, about thirty miles east of San Juan Capistrano.

Lake Perris State Recreation Area
(714) 657-0676

The 2,000-acre reservoir is the last storage area for the California Water Project. It has facilities for boaters, campers (432 sites), anglers, swimmers, rock climbers, and picnickers. Day-use boaters may need reservations to get in on many summer weekends. The lake is located eleven miles south of Riverside via State Route 60 or I-215.

Mount San Jacinto State Park and Wilderness
(714) 659-2607

This 13,500-acre park, most of which is wilderness, contains three mountain peaks higher than 10,000 feet. While many people hike in from trails on the west side of the park, others ride the Palm Springs Aerial Tramway 2.5 miles up the mountain. For hikers and backpackers, wilderness permits are required. The park has eighty-three sites. (See full description in Section 1, page 204.)

Palomar Mountain State Park
(619) 742-3462

The highlight here is the Mount Palomar Observatory, which sits atop the 6,100-foot mountain. The conifer forests that cover much of the 1,897-acre park are more like the Sierra Nevada to the north than the dry lowlands that surround the mountain. There are spectacular views of the Pacific when coastal fog is not present. The park is located off State Route 76, up State Route S6, then left on State Route S7 at the junction near the top of the mountain. There are thirty-one campsites. (See full description in Section 1, page 206.)

Picacho State Recreation Area
(619) 339-1360 or 393-3052

Eight miles of the lower Colorado River serve as this recreation area's eastern border. The park is seldom used during the hot summer months, but during the remainder of the year it is a good destination for boaters, hikers, anglers, and campers (fifty-nine sites). To reach Picacho, take the twenty-four-mile, mostly unpaved road north from Winterhaven near the Mexican border.

Providence Mountains State Recreation Area
(619) 389-2303 or 389-2281

This park is best known for its Mitchell Caverns Natural Preserve, but the limestone caves are only a small part of this 5,250-acre recreation area. Limited cavern tours are offered year-round except summer. No water is available in the six primitive campsites. The park is 100 miles east of Barstow, 17 miles from I-40 on Essex Road. (See full description in Section 1, page 207.)

Red Rock Canyon State Park
(805) 942-0662

The colorful rock formations in the 4,000-acre park served as a landmark during the early 1870s for twenty-mule-team freight wagons that stopped here for spring water. In recent times, Hollywood has filmed movies among the rock formations. The old 1890s gold rush stagecoach station now serves as park headquarters. The park is located twenty-five miles northeast of Mojave on State Route 14. There are fifty campsites. (See full description in Section 1, page 209.)

Saddleback Butte State Park
(805) 942-0662

A 3,641-foot-high granite capped butte sits a thousand feet higher than the surrounding Mojave Desert and offers spectacular views. Joshua trees, palm-like yuccas that grow to thirty feet in height, grace the park's 2,875 acres. The park entrance is on Avenue J East and 170th Street, seventeen miles east of Lancaster. There are fifty sites. (See full description in Section 1, page 211.)

Salton Sea State Recreation Area
(619) 393-3052 or 393-3059

One of the world's largest inland seas was accidentally created when a dike broke during the 1905 construction of the All-American Canal. The 360-square mile basin attracts boaters, water-skiers, and anglers looking to catch such ocean transplants as corvina, gulf croaker, and sargo. The visitor center is 25 miles southeast of Indio via State Route 111. There are 150 sites.

Silverwood Lake State Recreation Area
(619) 389-2281 or 389-2303

The State Water Project reservoir is located at an elevation of 3,350 feet in the San Bernardino Mountains. The park is reached via State Route 138, eleven miles east of I-15 or, alternately, twenty miles north of San Bernardino via State Routes 18 and 138. There are 136 campsites.

CHAPTER 11

NATIONAL PARKS

NATIONAL PARK SERVICE, WESTERN REGION
Building 201, Ft. Mason
San Francisco, CA 94123
(415) 556-0560

Everyone knows about the national parks, which receive far more publicity than most other federal and state agencies that cater to campers. As a result, campgrounds in the parks are frequently crowded, and camping at them is more like being in an outdoor motel than in a natural environment. With modern conveniences such as grocery stores, showers, Laundromats, and restaurants nearby it is difficult to call any outing "roughing it." Nevertheless, there are great attractions in the parks, and families flock to them every vacation season.

If you decide to head for one of the more popular parks during the busy seasons you should plan far ahead and make reservations through the proper agency to ensure a campsite.

On the whole, national monuments are less crowded than national parks, and the more isolated the park unit the more likely you will find a campsite without reservations.

One benefit of national parks is that most have one or more nonprofit educational institutes associated with them. These offer classes on the ecology and natural world of the parks, and most have offerings for the whole family to enjoy as they learn.

While some of the national park's campgrounds are on a first-come, first-served basis others are on a reservation system. For campground reservations at those national parks call (800) 365-2267.

The national parks in California most heavily used by campers include Yosemite, Sequoia, Kings Canyon, and Death Valley. Some that offer different, but outstanding sights, and that are much less crowded, are Lassen, Lava Beds, Joshua Tree, Pinnacles, and Mojave.

Channel Islands National Park
1901 Spinnaker Drive
Ventura, CA 93001
(805) 644-8262

Primitive camping with no developed facilities.

Death Valley National Monument
Highway 190
Death Valley, CA 92328
(619) 786-2331

This park features ten campgrounds with over 1,500 sites. Some campgrounds offer only primitive sites with few facilities, while others have complete facilities, including showers.

East Mojave Natural Preserve
c/o California Desert Information Center
831 Barstow Rd.
Barstow, CA 92311
(619) 256-8313

Four developed campgrounds with seventy-two sites.

Golden Gate National Recreation Area
Fort Mason, Building 201
San Francisco CA 94123
(415) 556-0560

An evening hike along the river is a great way to end a camping day.

Only backpacking camps.

Joshua Tree National Park
74485 National Monument Drive
Twentynine Palms, CA 92277
(619) 367-7511

Eight campgrounds with over 400 sites, plus three walk-in campgrounds with 22 sites.

Kings Canyon National Park
c/o Sequoia and Kings Canyon National Parks
Three Rivers, CA 93271
(209) 568-3341

Seven campgrounds with over 700 sites.

Lassen Volcanic National Park
38050 Highway 36 E
P.O. Box 100
Mineral, CA 96063
(916) 595-4444

Seven campgrounds with almost 500 sites.

Lava Beds National Monument
P.O. Box 867
Tulelake, CA 96134
(916) 667-2282

One campground with forty sites.

Pinnacles National Monument
Paicines, CA 95403
(408) 389-4485

One campground with twenty-four walk-in sites.

Point Reyes National Seashore
Bear Valley Road
Point Reyes Station, CA 94956
(415) 663-1092

Backpacking campgrounds only.

Redwood National Park
1111 Second Street
Crescent City, CA 95531
(707) 464-6101

Over 350 campsites in three state parks within the boundaries of the national park.

Santa Monica Mountains National Recreation Area
30401 Agoura Road, Suite 100
Agoura Hills, CA 91301
(818) 597-9192

Campgrounds in state and county parks within the boundaries of a recreation area.

Whiskey-Shasta-Trinity National Recreation Area
P.O. Box 188
Whiskeytown, CA 96095
(916) 241-6584

Almost 300 walk-in and trailer campsites in three campgrounds.

Yosemite National Park
P.O. Box 577
Yosemite National Park, CA 95389
(209) 372-0200

Seventeen campgrounds with almost 2,000 sites.

CHAPTER 12

U.S. FOREST SERVICE SITES

U.S. FOREST SERVICE, PACIFIC SOUTHWEST REGION
630 Sansome Street
San Francisco, CA 94111
(415) 705-2874

A lthough the USFS has more campsites than all the state and national parks in California combined, families are less likely to head for the forest service campgrounds for their vacations. This is unfortunate, especially for families who want to truly experience the outdoors.

Forest service campgrounds are less likely to be crowded, and there are generally far fewer services nearby. This does not mean that they don't provide the basics. All the campgrounds have defined campsites with fire rings and tables, and most have water in or near each campsite and toilets with running water.

Even those that have chemical toilets and no water are often located in beautiful areas where families who want to hike and fish in solitude can experience a restful and enjoyable vacation far away from the crowds found in more developed campgrounds. Another advantage of camping in the national forests is that you can camp anywhere on national forest land as long as you are away from defined recreation sites. All you have to do is locate a good level spot that meets your needs and set up camp. Of course you won't have the conveniences found at developed campgrounds, but you won't have to fight crowds either.

Reservations can be made for only a few forest service campgrounds, but you should call the forest supervisor or local ranger district to find out if reservations are necessary at the campground you are planning to use.

When you call also ask for a USFS map of that particular national forest. These maps not only indicate the location of all the campgrounds in the forest, they also are the only up-to-date maps that include all the forest service roads in the region. This will help you plan day outings from your campground. The following entries are arranged by National Forest and ranger districts within the forest.

ANGELES NATIONAL FOREST SUPERVISOR
701 North Santa Anita Avenue
Arcadia, CA 91006
(818) 574-5200

Arroyo Seco Ranger District
Oak Grove Park
Flintridge, CA 91011
(818) 790-1151

Eight campgrounds with over 300 sites.

Mt. Baldy Ranger District
100 North Wabash Avenue
Glendora, CA 91740
(818) 335-1251

Six campgrounds with almost 250 sites.

Saugus Ranger District
30800 Bouquet Canyon Road
Saugus, CA 91350
(805) 296-9710

Thirteen campgrounds with over 200 sites.

Tujunga Ranger District
12371 North Little Tujunga Canyon Road
San Fernando, CA 91342
(818) 899-1900

Eight campgrounds with about 200 sites.

Valyemo Ranger District
Valyemo Road
P.O. Box 15
Valyemo, CA 93563
(805) 944-2187

Eighteen campgrounds with almost 300 sites.

CLEVELAND NATIONAL FOREST SUPERVISOR
10845 Rancho Bernardo Road, Suite 200
San Diego, CA 92127
(619) 673-6180

Descanso Ranger District
3348 Alpine Boulevard
Alpine, CA 92001
(619) 445-6235

Five campgrounds with almost 300 sites.

Palomar Ranger District
1634 Black Canyon Road
Ramona, CA 92065
(619) 788-0250

Five campgrounds with over 200 sites.

Trabuco Ranger District
1147 East Sixth Street
Corona, CA 91719
(714) 736-1811

Five campgrounds with almost 120 sites.

ELDORADO NATIONAL FOREST SUPERVISOR
100 Forni Road
Placerville, CA 95667
(916) 622-5061

Amador Ranger District
26820 Silver Drive and Highway 88
Star Route 3
Pioneer, CA 95666
(209) 295-4251

Fourteen campgrounds with over 300 sites.

Eldorado National Forest Information Center
3070 Camino Heights Drive
Camino, CA 95709
(916) 644-6048

Georgetown Ranger District
7600 Wentworth Springs Road
Georgetown, CA 95634
(916) 333-4312

Four campgrounds with 120 sites.

Pacific Ranger District
Pollock Pines, CA 95726
(916) 644-2349

Eleven campgrounds with over 550 sites.

Placerville Ranger District
3491 Carson Court
Placerville, CA 95667
(916) 644-2324

Four campgrounds with almost 100 sites.

INYO NATIONAL FOREST SUPERVISOR
873 North Main Street
Bishop, CA 93514
(619) 873-5841

Mammoth Ranger District
P.O. Box 148
Mammoth Lakes, CA 93546
(619) 924-5500

Fifteen campgrounds with over 750 sites.

Mono Lake Ranger District
P.O. Box 429
Lee Vining, CA 93541
(619) 647-6525

Sixteen campgrounds with 475 sites.

Mt. Whitney Ranger District
P.O. Box 8
Lone Pine, CA 93545
(619) 876-5542

Ten campgrounds with over 250 sites.

White Mountain Ranger District
798 North Main Street
Bishop, CA 93514
(619) 873-2525

Sixteen campgrounds with almost 350 sites.

California gulls feed on brine shrimp in Mono Lake.

KLAMATH NATIONAL FOREST SUPERVISOR
1312 Fairlane Road
Yreka, CA 96097
(916) 842-6131

Goosenest Ranger District
37805 Highway 97
Macdowel, CA 96058
(916) 398-4391

Three campgrounds with forty-one sites.

Happy Camp Ranger District
Highway 96
P.O. Box 377
Happy Camp, CA 96039
(916) 493-2243

Two campgrounds with twenty-two sites.

Oak Knoll Ranger District
22541 Highway 96
Klamath River, CA 96050
(916) 465-2241

Six campgrounds with eighty sites.

Salmon River Ranger District
Highway 3
P.O. Box 280
Etna, CA 96027
(916) 467-5757

Seven campgrounds with seventy-five sites.

Scott River Ranger District
11263 North Highway 3
Fort Jones, CA 96032
(916) 468-5351

Six campgrounds with eighty sites.

Ukonom Ranger District
P.O. Drawer 410
Orleans, CA 95556
(916) 627-3291

Two campgrounds with fifty-six sites.

LAKE TAHOE BASIN MANAGEMENT UNIT
870 Emerald Bay Road, Suite 1
South Lake Tahoe, CA 96150
(916) 573-2600

Five campgrounds with 360 sites.

LASSEN NATIONAL FOREST SUPERVISOR
55 South Sacramento Street
Susanville, CA 96130
(916) 257-2151

Almanor Ranger District
900 East Highway 36
P.O. Box 767
Chester, CA 96020
(916) 258-2141

Twenty-two campgrounds with almost 450 sites.

Eagle Lake Ranger District
c/o United States Forest Service
55 South Sacramento Street
Susanville, CA 96130
(916) 257-2595

Seven campgrounds with almost 400 sites.

Hat Creek Ranger District
P.O. Box 220
Fall River Mills, CA 96028
(916) 336-5521

Six campgrounds with over 175 sites.

LOS PADRES NATIONAL FOREST SUPERVISOR
6144 Calle Real
Goleta, CA 93117
(805) 683-6711

Monterey Ranger District
406 South Mildred
King City, CA 93930
(408) 385-5434

Ten campgrounds with almost 200 sites.

Mt. Pinos Ranger District
Star Route, Box 400
Frazier Park, CA 93225
(805) 245-3731

Twenty-two campgrounds with almost 300 sites.

Ojai Ranger District
1190 East Ojai Avenue
Ojai, CA 93023
(805) 646-4348

Nine campgrounds with almost 200 sites.

Santa Barbara Ranger District
Star Route, Los Prietos
Santa Barbara, CA 93105
(805) 967-3481

Eleven campgrounds with 175 sites.

Santa Lucia Ranger District
1616 North Carlotti Drive
Santa Maria, CA 93454
(805) 925-9538

Eighteen campgrounds with 155 sites.

MENDOCINO NATIONAL FOREST SUPERVISOR
420 East Laurel Street

Willows, CA 95988
(916) 934-3316

Corning Ranger District
22000 Corning Road
P.O. Box 1019
Corning, CA 96021
(916) 824-5196

Nine campgrounds with fifty-five sites.

Covelo Ranger District
Route 1, Box 62-C
Covelo, CA 95428
(707) 983-6118

Three campgrounds with forty-six sites.

Stonyford Ranger District
Stites Ladoga Road
Stonyford, CA 95979
(916) 963-3128

Twelve campgrounds with 170 sites.

Upper Lake Ranger District
Middlecreek Road
P.O. Box 96
Upper Lake, CA 95485
(707) 275-2361

Eight campgrounds with 175 sites.

MODOC NATIONAL FOREST SUPERVISOR
441 North Main Street
Alturas, CA 96101
(916) 233-5811

Big Valley Ranger District
P.O. Box 159
Adin, CA 96006
(916) 299-3215

Five campgrounds with fifty-one sites.

Devil's Garden Ranger District
P.O. Box 5
Canby, CA 96015
(916) 233-4611

Two campgrounds with twenty-one sites.

Doublehead Ranger District
P.O. Box 369
Tulelake, CA 96134
(916) 667-2247

Three campgrounds with seventy-two sites.

Warner Mountain Ranger District
P.O. Box 220
Cedarville, CA 96104
(916) 279-6116

Nine campgrounds with 128 sites.

PLUMAS NATIONAL FOREST SUPERVISOR
159 Lawrence Street
P.O. Box 11500
Quincy, CA 95971
(916) 283-2050

Beckworth Ranger District/Mohawk Ranger Station
Mohawk Road
P.O. Box 7
Blairsden, CA 96013
(916) 836-2575

Six campgrounds with 234 sites.

Greenville Ranger District
410 Main Street
P.O. Box 329
Greenville, CA 95947
(916) 284-7126

Three campgrounds with almost 200 sites.

La Porte Ranger District/Challenge Ranger Station
10087 La Porte Road
P.O. Drawer 369
Challenge, CA 95925
(916) 675-2462

Three campgrounds with almost 200 sites.

Milford Ranger District/Laufman Ranger Station
Milford Grade
Milford, CA 96121
(916) 253-2223

Eight campgrounds with 222 sites.

Oroville Ranger District
875 Mitchell Avenue
Oroville, CA 95965
(916) 534-6500

Eight campgrounds with ninety-five sites.

Quincy Ranger District
39696 Highway 70
Quincy, CA 95971
(916) 283-0555

Seven campgrounds with eighty-six sites.

SAN BERNARDINO NATIONAL FOREST SUPERVISOR
1824 Commercenter Circle
San Bernardino, CA 92408
(714) 383-5588

Arrowhead Ranger District
State Highway 18
Rimforest, CA 92378
(714) 337-2444

Four campgrounds with 185 sites.

Big Bear Ranger District
P.O. Box 290
Fawnskin, CA 92333
(714) 866-3437

Seven campgrounds with over 250 sites.

Cajon Ranger District and Lytle Creek Ranger Station
1209 Lytle Creek Road, Star Route, Box 100
Fontana, CA 92336
(714) 887-2576

One campground with forty-four sites.

San Gorgonio Ranger District
Mill Creek Station
34701 Mill Creek Road
Mentone, CA 92359
(714) 794-1123

Four campgrounds with 225 sites.

San Jacinto Ranger District
Idyllwild Ranger Station
P.O. Box 518
Idyllwild, CA 92349
(714) 659-2117

Seven campgrounds with over 130 sites.

SEQUOIA NATIONAL FOREST SUPERVISOR
900 West Grand Avenue
Porterville, CA 93257
(209) 784-1500

Cannell Meadow Ranger District
P.O. Box 6105, Whitney Road
Kernville, CA 93238
(619) 376-3781

Ten campgrounds with almost 450 sites.

Greenhorn Ranger District
15701 Highway 178
P.O. Box 6129
Bakersfield, CA 93386
(805) 861-4212

Five campgrounds with eighty sites.

Hot Springs Ranger District
Route 4, Box 548
43474 Mountain Road 50
Hot Springs, CA 93207
(805) 548-6503

Nine campgrounds with ninety-five sites.

Hume Lake Ranger District
35860 East Kings Canyon Road
Dunlap, CA 93621
(209) 338-2251

Eleven campgrounds with almost 300 sites.

Tule Ranger District
32588 Highway 190
Springville, CA 93265
(209) 539-2607

Six campgrounds with almost 150 sites.

SHASTA-TRINITY NATIONAL FOREST SUPERVISOR
2400 Washington Avenue
Redding, CA 96001
(916) 246-5222

Big Bar Ranger District
Star Route 1, Box 10
Big Bar, CA 96010
(916) 623-6106

Eight campgrounds with 110 sites.

Hayfork Ranger District
P.O. Box 159
Hayfork, CA 96041
(916) 628-5227

Four campgrounds with fifty sites.

McCloud Ranger District
P.O. Box 1620
McCloud, CA 96057
(916) 964-2184

Five campgrounds with 110 sites.

Mt. Shasta Ranger District
204 West Alma
Mt. Shasta, CA 96067
(916) 926-4511

Seven campgrounds with fifty-seven sites.

Shasta Lake Ranger District
14225 Holiday Road
Redding, CA 96003
(916) 275-1587

Thirty-three campgrounds with 530 sites.

Weaverville Ranger District
P.O. Box 1190
Weaverville, CA 96093
(916) 623-2131

Twenty-three campgrounds with almost 600 sites.

Yolla Bolla Ranger District
Platina, CA 96076
(916) 352-4211

Seven campgrounds with over seventy-five sites.

SIERRA NATIONAL FOREST SUPERVISOR
Federal Building

1600 Tollhouse Road
Clovis, CA 93612
(209) 487-5155

Kings River Ranger District
34849 Maxon Road
Sanger, CA 93657
(209) 855-8321

Twelve campgrounds with 325 sites.

Mariposa Ranger District
41969 Highway 41
Oakhurst, CA 93644
(209) 683-4665

Sixteen campgrounds with over 400 sites.

Minarets Ranger District
North Fork, CA 93643
(209) 877-2218

Thirteen campgrounds with over 175 sites.

Pineridge Ranger District
P.O. Box 300
Shaver Lake, CA 93664
(209) 841-3311

Twenty campgrounds with almost 600 sites.

SIX RIVERS NATIONAL FOREST SUPERVISOR
1330 Bayshore Way
Eureka, CA 95501-3834
(707) 442-1721

Lower Trinity Ranger District
P.O. Box 668
Willow Creek, CA 95573
(916) 629-2118

Three campgrounds with 100 sites.

Ferns come out in lush growth after the first winter rains.

Mad River Ranger District
Star Route, Box 300
Bridgeville, CA 95526
(707) 574-6233

Three campgrounds with over 80 sites.

Orleans Ranger District
Drawer B
Orleans, CA 95556
(916) 627-3291

Four campgrounds with seventy-five sites.

Smith River National Recreation Area
P.O. Box 228
Gasquet, CA 95543
(707) 457-3131

Four campgrounds with 110 sites.

STANSILAUS NATIONAL FOREST SUPERVISOR
19777 Greenley Road
Sonora, CA 95370
(209) 532-3671

Calaveras Ranger District
Highway 4
P.O. Box 500
Hathaway Pines, CA 95233
(209) 795-1381

Fourteen campgrounds with over 230 sites.

Groveland Ranger District
Highway 120-Star Route
P.O. Box 75 G
Groveland, CA 95321
(209) 962-7825

Nine campgrounds with 150 sites.

Mi-Wok Ranger District
Highway 108E
P.O. Box 100
Mi-Wok Village, CA 95346
(209) 586-3234

Summit Ranger District
Highway 108E at Pinecrest, Star Route, Box 1295
Sonora, CA 95370
(209) 965-3434

Summit and Mi-Wok jointly administer twenty-one campgrounds with almost 750 sites.

TAHOE NATIONAL FOREST SUPERVISOR
Highway 49, 631 Coyote Street
P.O. Box 6063
Nevada City, CA 95959
(916) 265-4531

Downieville Ranger District
15924 Highway 49
Camptonville, CA 95922
(916) 288-3231

Twenty-one campgrounds with almost 400 sites.

Foresthill Ranger District
22830 Auburn-Foresthill Road
Foresthill, CA 95631
(916) 367-2224

Ten campgrounds with over 230 sites.

Nevada City Ranger District
Highway 49, 631 Coyote Street
P.O. Box 6063
Nevada City, CA 95959
(916) 265-4538

Thirteen campgrounds with 220 sites.

Sierraville Ranger District
Highway 89
P.O. Box 95
Sierraville, CA 96126
(916) 994-3401

Eleven campgrounds with almost 250 sites.

Truckee Ranger District
P.O. Box 909
Truckee, CA 95734
(916) 587-3558

Eleven campgrounds with over 700 sites.

TOYIABE NATIONAL FOREST SUPERVISOR
1200 Franklin Way
Sparks, NV 89431
(702) 331-6444

Bridgeport Ranger District
Highway 395
P.O. Box 595
Bridgeport, CA 93517
(619) 932-7070

Thirteen campgrounds with almost 500 sites.

INDEX

A

Ahjumawi Lava Springs State Park, 239
Almanor Ranger District, 275
Alturas Resource Area, 226
Amador Ranger District, 272
American River, 89
American River Parkway, 89
Andrew Molera State Park, 245
Angeles National Forest, 173, 270
Antelope Valley, 211
Anza-Borrego Desert State Park, 193, 195, 257
Arcata Resource Area, 227
Armstrong Redwoods State Preserve, 21
Army Corps of Engineers, 219
Arrowhead Ranger District, 279
Arroyo Seco Ranger District, 270
Auburn State Recreation Area, 240
Austin Creek State Recreation Area, 21, 234
Avenue of the Giants, 32

B

Bale Grist mill State Historic Park, 74

Banana Slug Derby, 46
Barstow Desert Information Center, 225
Barstow Resource Area, 225
Bears, 7, 8
Beckworth Ranger District/Mohawk Ranger Station, 278
Benbow Lake State Recreation Area, 234
Big Bar Ranger District, 281
Big Basin Redwoods State Park, 125, 245
Big Bear Ranger District, 280
Big Sur, 123, 132
Big Sur River, 138
Big Valley Ranger District, 277
Bigfoot country, 57
Bishop Resource Area, 224
Black Butte Lake, 220
Bodega Head, 60
Boggs Mountain State Forest, 229
Bothe-Napa Valley State Park, 73, 240
Brannan Island State Recreation Area, 75, 250
Bridgeport Ranger District, 287
Bumpass Hell, 97
Bureau of Land Management, 223
Butano State Park, 127, 246

C

Cajon Ranger District, 280
Calaveras Big Trees State Park, 147, 250
Calaveras Ranger District, 285
Caliente Resource Area, 224
California State Forests, 229
California State Parks, 233
Campground reservations, 12
Camping tips, 1
Cannell Meadow Ranger District, 280
Carpinteria State Beach, 254
Carson River, 153, 174
Cascades, 71
Castle Crags, 115
Castle Crags State Park, 76, 240
Caswell Memorial State Park, 145, 251
Central Coast Camping, 123
Central Inland Camping, 143
Channel Islands National park, 183, 264
China Camp State Park, 246
Cima Dome, 208
Clear Lake, 229
Clear Lake Resource Area, 227
Clear Lake State Park, 240
Cleveland National Forest, 197, 271
Clothing, 10
Coastal redwoods, 19
Colonel Allensworth State Historic Park, 252
Colorado Desert, 202
Colusa-Sacramento River State Recreation Area, 78, 241
Cooking accessories, 11
Corning Ranger District, 277
Covelo Ranger District, 277
Cuyamaca Rancho State Park, 199, 258

D

D.L. Bliss State Park, 80, 241
Death Valley, 145
Death Valley Encampment, 151
Death Valley Fall Festival, 151
Death Valley National Park, 149, 264
Del Norte Coast Redwoods State Park, 23, 234
Descanso Ranger District, 271
Desolation Valley, 118
Devil's Garden Ranger District, 278
Doheny State Beach, 254
Donner Lake, 82
Donner Memorial State Park, 82, 242
Doublehead Ranger District, 278
Downieville Ranger District, 286

E

Eagle Lake Ranger District, 275
Eagle Lake Resource Area, 226
Earth Day in the Desert, 197
East Mojave Natural Preserve, 264
Eastman Lake, 220
Eel River, 33, 46, 56, 63
El Capitan State Beach, 255
El Centro Resource Area, 225
El Dorado National Forest, 83, 272
El Dorado National Forest Information Center, 272
Elephant seals, 123
Emerald Bay, 81
Emerald Bay State Park, 87, 242
Englebright Lake, 220

Equipment checklist, 9
Eureka, 38

F
Feather River, 113
First aid kits, 6
Fishing gear, 5
Folsom Lake State Recreation Area, 88, 242
Folsom Resource Area, 224
Food, 4
Foresthill Ranger District, 286
Fort Bragg, 36
Fort Ross Historic Park, 234
Fremont Peak State Park, 246

G
Garberville, 47
Gaviota State Park, 247
General Grant Grove, 160
George J. Hatfield State Recreation Area, 252
Georgetown Ranger District, 272
Giardia, 6
Glacier, 156
Gold Rush country, 143, 172
Golden Gate National Recreation Area, 26, 264
Goosenest Ranger District, 274
Great Valley Tule Fog Fete, 147
Greenhorn Ranger District, 281
Greenville Ranger District, 278
Grizzly Creek Redwoods State park, 28, 235
Groveland Ranger District, 285
Grover Hot Springs State Park, 151, 243

H
Happy Camp Ranger District, 274
Harbor seals, 63
Harry A. Merlo State Recreation Area, 235
Hat Creek Ranger District, 275
Hayfork Ranger District, 282
Health and safety, 6
Hendy Woods State Park, 30, 235
Henry Cowell Redwoods State Park, 129, 247
Henry W. Coe State Park, 154, 252
Hensley Lake, 221
Hiking boots, 5
Hollister Hills State Vehicle Recreation Area, 247
Hollister Resource Area, 224
Hot Creek, 93
Hot Springs Ranger District, 281
Hot springs, 153
Humboldt Lagoons State Park, 235
Humboldt Redwoods State Park, 31, 235
Hume Lake Ranger District, 281

I
Indian Grinding Rock State Historic Park, 155, 252
Inyo National Forest, 156, 272
Island Packers, 183

J
Jackson State Forest, 230
Jedediah Smith Redwoods State Park, 34, 236
John Muir Trail, 156, 158, 160
Johnsville, 109

Joshua Tree National Park,
193, 202, 265
Juanita Lake, 91

K
Kangaroo Lake, 91
Kern River, 164, 166
Kings Canyon National Park,
160, 265
Kings River, 164, 166
Kings River Ranger District,
283
Klamath National Forest, 90,
274
Klamath River, 56, 90
Kruse Rhododendron State
Reserve, 50
Kule Loklo, 43

L
La Porte Ranger District, 279
Lake Elsinore State Recreation
Area, 258
Lake Isabella, 221
Lake Kaweah, 221
Lake Mendocino, 221
Lake Oroville State Recreation
Area, 243
Lake Perris State Recreation
Area, 258
Lake Pillsbury, 106
Lake Sonoma, 221
Lake Tahoe, 80, 117
Lake Tahoe Basin Manage-
ment Unit, 275
Lassen National Forest, 92, 275
Lassen Volcanic National
park, 93, 95, 265
Latour State Forest, 231
Lava Beds National Monu-
ment, 98, 266
Layered clothes, 3
Leo Carillo State Beach, 186,
255

Little River, 69
Logging History Days, 69
Loon Lake, 85
Los Padres National Forest,
131, 276
Lost children, 6
Lost Coast of California, 53
Lower Bear Reservoir, 85
Lower Trinity Ranger District,
283

M
MacKerricher State Park, 36,
236
Mad River, 56
Mad River Ranger District,
284
Malakoff Diggins State His-
toric Park, 99, 243
Malibu Creek State Park, 255
Mammoth Lakes Basin, 157
Mammoth Ranger District, 273
Manchester State Beach, 236
Marble Mountains, 90, 116
Marin Headlands, 26, 27
Mariposa Ranger District, 283
Martis Creek Lake, 221
McArthur-Burney Heritage
Days, 103
McArthur-Burney Falls
Memorial State Park, 102,
244
McCloud Ranger District, 282
McConnell State Recreation
Area, 253
Mendocino National Forest,
103, 276
Mi-Wok Ranger District, 285
Migrating salmon, 53, 58, 129,
146
Milford Ranger District, 279
Millerton Lake State Recre-
ation Area, 253
Minarets Ranger District, 283

Mineral King Valley, 167
Mitchell Caverns Natural Preserve, 207
Modoc National Forest, 106, 277
Modoc Plateau, 93
Modoc War, 98
Mojave Desert, 202
Mojave Natural Preserve, 266
Mono Lake, 158
Mono Lake Ranger District, 273
Montana de Oro State Park, 134, 247
Monterey Ranger District, 276
Morro Bay Area State Parks, 133
Morro Bay State Park, 247
Morro Strand Beach, 248
Mount Diablo State Park, 162, 253
Mount San Jacinto State Park and Wilderness, 204, 259
Mount Tamalpais State Park, 248
Mountain lion, 7, 8, 200
Mountain Home State Forest, 231
Mt. Baldy Ranger District, 270
Mt. Pinos Ranger District, 276
Mt. Shasta, 76, 114, 115, 162
Mt. Shasta Ranger District, 282
Mt. Tamalpais, 26
Mt. Whitney, 156, 160
Mt. Whitney Ranger District, 273
Mushrooms, 130

N
National Park Service, 263
Native American villages, 40, 43, 155
Navarro River, 30
Needles Resource Area, 225

Nevada City Ranger District, 286
New Hogan Lake, 222
North Coast Camping, 20
North Inland Camping, 71

O
Oak riparian forest, 145
Oak Knoll Ranger District, 274
Ohlone Days, 130
Ojai Ranger District, 276
Old Mill Days, 74
Orleans Ranger District, 284
Oroville Ranger District, 279

P
Pacific Crest Trail, 76, 103, 115, 156, 180, 182, 212
Pacific Ranger District, 272
Pajaro Coast State Park and State Beaches, 248
Palm Springs Aerial Tramway, 205
Palm Springs-South Coast Resource Area, 225
Palomar Mountain State Park, 206, 259
Palomar Observatory, 198
Palomar Ranger District, 271
Patrick's Point State Park, 38, 236
Pelican rookery, 185
Personal gear, 10
Pfeiffer Big Sur State Park, 136, 249
Picacho State Recreation Area, 259
Pine Flat Lake, 222
Pineridge Ranger District, 283
Pinnacles National Monument, 138, 266
Pismo State Beach, 249
Placerville Ranger District, 272

Plumas Eureka State Park, 109, 244
Plumas National Forest, 112, 278
Point Magu State Park, 187, 256
Point Reyes Field Seminars, 43
Point Reyes National Seashore, 41, 266
Portola State Park, 140, 249
Prairie Creek Redwoods State Park, 44, 237
Providence Mountains State Recreation Area, 207, 259
Providence Mountains, 193
Pygmy forests, 49, 68, 230

Q
Quincy Ranger District, 279

R
Rattlesnakes, 7, 67, 162
Red Rock Canyon State Park, 209, 260
Redding Resource Area, 227
Redwood National and State Parks Field Seminars, 26, 29, 34, 36, 40, 46, 55
Redwood National Park, 25, 266
Refugio State Beach, 256
Richardson Grove State Park, 46, 237
Ridgecrest Resource Area, 225
Roosevelt elk, 44, 54
Russian Gulch State Park, 237
Russian River, 21, 60

S
Sacramento National Wildlife Refuge, 80
Sacramento/San Joaquin Delta, 75, 146
Saddleback Butte State Park, 211, 260

Salmon River, 90
Salmon River Ranger District, 274
Salt Point State Park, 48, 238
Salton Sea State Recreation Area, 260
Samuel P. Taylor State Park, 51, 249
San Bernardino National Forest, 213, 279
San Clemente State Beach, 256
San Diego Coast State Parks and State Beaches, 183, 256
San Elijo State Beach, 190
San Francisco Bay Region, 26
San Gabriel Mountains, 181
San Gorgonio Ranger District, 280
San Jacinto Ranger District, 280
San Lorenzo River, 129, 130
San Luis Reservoir State Recreation Area, 254
San Onofre State Beach, 257
San Simeon State Park, 250
sandhill crane, 73
Santa Barbara Ranger District, 276
Santa Cruz Mountains, 127
Santa Cruz Museum of natural History, 130
Santa Lucia Ranger District, 276
Santa Monica Area State Beaches, 257
Santa Monica Mountains National Recreation Area, 179, 191, 266
Saugus Ranger District, 270
Scott River, 90
Scott River Ranger District, 274
Sea lions, 184
Sea otter, 138

Sequoia National Forest, 164, 280

Sequoia National Park, 167

Shasta Lake Ranger District, 282

Shasta-Trinity National Forest, 114, 281

Shelter, 9

Sierra Buttes, 119

Sierra National Forest, 169, 282

Sierra Nevada, 71, 143

Sierraville Ranger District, 286

Silverwood Lake State Recreation Area, 261

Sinkyone Wilderness State Park, 53, 238

Siskiyou Mountains, 59

Six Rivers National Forest 55, 58, 283

Sleeping bags, 9

Sleeping gear, 3

Smith River, 34, 56

Smith River National Recreation Area, 58, 284

Sonoma Coast State Beach, 60, 238

Sonora Pass, 173

South Carslbad State Beach, 190

South Coast Camping, 179

South Inland Camping, 193

Standish-Hickey State Recreation Area, 63, 238

Stanislaus National Forest, 172, 285

Stanislaus River, 145, 148

Stellar sea lions, 123

Stonyford Ranger District, 277

Success Lake, 222

Sugar Pine Point State Park, 117, 244

Sugarloaf Ridge State Park, 65, 239

Sumeg, 40

Summit Ranger District, 285

Surprise Resource Area, 226

T

Tahoe Basin, 80, 117

Tahoe National Forest, 119, 285

Tahoe State Recreation Area, 244

Tents, 9

Toiyabe National Forest, 173, 286

Topanga State Park, 192

Trabuco Ranger District, 271

Trinity Alps, 90, 115

Trinity River, 56

Truckee Ranger District, 286

Tujunga Ranger District, 271

Tule elk, 43

Tule Ranger District, 281

tundra swan, 73

Tuolumne Meadows, 176

Tuolumne River, 172

Turlock Lake State Recreation Area, 254

U

U.S. Forest Service, 269

Ukonom Ranger District, 275

Upper Lake Ranger District, 277

V

Valyemo Ranger District, 271

Van Damme State Park, 67, 239

Van Duzen River, 28, 56

Ventana Wilderness, 136

Ventura Area State Beaches, 257

Vikingsholm, 87

W

Warner Mountain Ranger
District, 278
Warner Mountains, 107
Waterfalls, 125, 127, 149, 183
Weaverville Ranger District,
282
Western States Trail, 89
Westport-Union Landing State
Park, 239
Whale watching, 37, 43, 55, 62,
123, 186
Whiskey-Shasta-Trinity
National Recreation Area,
266
White water rafting, 166, 172
White Mountain Ranger Dis-
trict, 274
Wild Horse Mesa, 208
Wildflowers, 66, 71, 120, 149,
175, 193, 196, 202, 210
Wildlife encounters, 7
Woods Lake, 85
Woodson Bridge State Recre-
ation Area, 245

Y

Yellow-billed cukcoo, 79
Yolla Bolla Ranger District,
282
Yosemite, 71
Yosemite National Park, 167,
175, 267